Powerful Partnerships

Twenty Crime Prevention Strategies That Work for Refugees, Law Enforcement, and Communities

TAKE A BITE OUT OF CRIME®

National Crime Prevention Council

Publication Funded by
Bureau of Justice Assistance
Office of Justice Programs ▪ U.S. Department of Justice

U.S. DEPARTMENT OF HEALTH AND HUMAN SERVICES
Administration for Children and Families
Office of Refugee Resettlement

This publication was developed by the National Crime Prevention Council (NCPC) through funding from the Office of Refugee Resettlement, U.S. Department of Health and Human Services, under Interagency Agreement #95-DD-BX-K012 with the Bureau of Justice Assistance, Office of Justice Programs, U.S. Department of Justice. Opinions are those of NCPC or cited sources and do not necessarily reflect U.S. Department of Justice policy or positions. The Bureau of Justice Assistance is a component of the Office of Justice Programs, which also includes the Bureau of Justice Statistics, the National Institute of Justice, the Office of Juvenile Justice and Delinquency Prevention, and the Office for Victims of Crime.

TAKE A BITE OUT OF CRIME

The National Crime Prevention Council is a private, nonprofit tax-exempt [501(c)(3)] organization whose principal mission is to enable people to prevent crime and build safer, more caring communities. NCPC publishes books, kits of camera-ready program materials, posters, and informational and policy reports on a variety of crime prevention and community-building subjects. NCPC offers training, technical assistance, and national focus for crime prevention: it acts as secretariat for the Crime Prevention Coalition of America, more than 117 national, federal, and state organizations committed to preventing crime. It also operates demonstration programs and takes a major leadership role in youth crime prevention. NCPC manages the McGruff "Take A Bite Out Of Crime" public service advertising campaign, which is substantially funded by the Bureau of Justice Assistance, Office of Justice Programs, U.S. Department of Justice. Proceeds from the sale of materials funded by public sources are used to help support NCPC's work on the National Citizens' Crime Prevention Campaign.

Printed in the United States of America
June 1998

National Crime Prevention Council
1700 K Street, NW, Second Floor
Washington, DC 20006-3817
202-466-6272
http://www.weprevent.org

ISBN 0-934513-74-0

Table of Contents

I

HOW CAN POWERFUL PARTNERSHIPS HELP ME?

II

TWENTY SUCCESSFUL PARTNERSHIP PROGRAMS

III

RESOURCES

Key Program Elements Index

Looking for a program to fill a particular need in your community? The following Key Program Elements Guide lists common program components and identifies which programs contain them. The numbers refer to the strategy number in the book where the program descriptions are located.

Acknowledgments

Powerful Partnerships would not have been possible without the contributions of a great many people. The document was produced for Outreach to New Americans (ONA), a project initiated and sustained through a partnership of the National Crime Prevention Council (NCPC); the Office of Refugee Resettlement (ORR), U.S. Department of Health and Human Services; and the Bureau of Justice Assistance (BJA), Office of Justice Programs, U.S. Department of Justice. A true partnership on many levels — a national nonprofit and many federal, state, and local agencies.

At NCPC, John A. Calhoun, executive director, and Maria Nagorski, deputy executive director, have provided guidance and enthusiastic support of both ONA and the production of this book. As program manager, Lyn McCoy directed the writing of *Powerful Partnerships* and provides general management of ONA with the extremely able assistance of Marouf Jwanmery and Weris Jama, program specialists. Interns Lori Doss and Jane Blackburn worked tirelessly gathering information for *Powerful Partnerships* and contributing to the document drafts. Invaluable editing and production expertise was provided by NCPC's Jean O'Neil, editor-in-chief, Judy Kirby, managing editor, and Marty Pociask, production director.

ORR's director Lavinia Limon is a firm believer in the importance of crime prevention and refugee/law enforcement partnerships and has been a staunch supporter of ONA. Anna Mary Portz, project officer, unflaggingly provides guidance in a hundred great and small ways, while the remaining ORR staff enthusiastically facilitate the work of the project by linking ONA services with the communities they serve.

At BJA, Nancy E. Gist, director, Robert H. Brown, Jr., chief, crime prevention branch, and Sasha Cohen, program specialist, encourage and build agency support for the project. Louise Lucas, project officer, was an advocate and an ardent supporter, always ready to respond to questions and requests from project staff.

The real heroes of this effort are the contact people for the 20 successful partnership programs, who not only guided the creation of these excellent programs, but also endured countless telephone calls and faxes from NCPC staff and volunteers gathering information, photographs, and quotations.

And to all those who reviewed *Powerful Partnerships* and gave us frank advice to help make the book as useful as possible to a variety of readers, you have our deepest appreciation.

Finally, hearty thanks go to the Georgian Human Relations Commission, Georgia State University, the Georgia Department of Human Resources, the Multicultural Crime Task Force, Asian Community Services, Inc., the Metropolitan Atlanta Crime Commission, and Georgia Advocates for Battered Women and Children for creating the excellent cultural fact sheet series, which were the source of the scenarios used at the beginning of this book, and to The Bridging the Gap Project, Inc., for making the fact sheets available to us.

SECTION I

How Can *Powerful Partnerships* Help Me?

How Can *Powerful Partnerships* Help Me?

Crime and victimization are problems that concern everyone in this country, but they have an especially devastating impact on our newly arrived residents—refugees.* Refugees usually won't seek help; they fear and mistrust people in uniform because of traumatic experiences in their homelands and during their escapes. At the same time, law enforcement officers often don't know how to communicate with refugees. On the part of both, there is often a feeling of uncertainty and frustration, sometimes even hostility.

Take a look at three actual events that took place in various parts of the country.

A refugee family is robbed at gunpoint, in their own neighborhood, by Asian gang members. They do not call the police for three reasons: they fear reprisals from the gang, language barriers mean they cannot effectively communicate with the police, and they fear the police.

Fear—leading to isolation and possible ongoing victimization.

Two refugee women were in an accident and taken to a hospital emergency room. The husband of one woman went to the hospital to find out about this wife. He did not speak English well, and when he tried to speak to the police officer there, he was told to sit down. Because he was so worried about his wife, he tried again to speak to the officer, this time grasping the officer's arm. The police officer, misunderstanding the husband's intentions, took the action as a threat and handcuffed him.

Misunderstanding—leading to inappropriate detention.

A 12-year-old girl is stealing money from family members and has even "borrowed" her parents' credit cards without permission. The parents fear using physical punishment to discipline her because they have been told it

---

* The National Crime Prevention Council's (NCPC) project, Outreach to New Americans, is funded by the Office of Refugee Resettlement (ORR) to help communities establish and maintain partnerships between refugees and law enforcement for crime and victimization prevention. Therefore, this book focuses on refugees. However, these ideas, techniques, and strategies will be useful to law enforcement who want to work with others newly arrived in this country, as well as to newcomers who are interested in working with law enforcement.

is illegal in this country and the authorities will take their child away. In desperation, they call 911. They have been told that, in America, the police are here to help. They hope for advice or counseling, but the police refer the case to Juvenile Court. The parents are deemed neglectful because they're not disciplining their daughter, and the girl is removed from her home and placed in foster care. There is no offer of counseling; the parents feel humiliated, angry, and betrayed by the system that was supposed to help them.

Lack of knowledge and communication—leading to anger and increased isolation.

These examples demonstrate the many reasons law enforcement and other authorities should work with newly arrived populations to ensure that refugees learn about their rights and responsibilities, the laws and legal system, and the resources available to them.

In communities where refugees have become essential partners in community crime prevention and refugees and law enforcement have begun working together, misunderstandings have become the exception rather than the rule.

The results of such cross-cultural problem solving are quite impressive. Law enforcement staff and refugees build communication and trust. Community conflicts are prevented or quickly resolved. Police are better able to do their jobs. And refugees begin to feel a part of their new community.

A refugee teenager attends the first day at his new school. Injured by a gunshot wound to his leg two years earlier during the war in his own country, he walks with a noticeable limp. At the end of the day, he finds himself surrounded by a group of his new schoolmates, all American-born boys, who call him names and beat him up because he is different. This treatment escalates and is extended to his younger siblings. Their mother tries to intervene, but the bullies also assault her. Local law enforcement is contacted. Officers identify the leaders and arrest them. The boys' parents (whom the police find to be encouraging their sons' behavior) are admonished. But the police don't stop there. They improve patrols in the area and work with school officials to educate students about the rights of newcomers and to punish students who do not respect the rules or the refugees. As a result, not only is a bullying situation resolved, but the refugee families in this neighborhood feel more secure.

Cooperation and problem solving fix causes, not just symptoms of problems.

Powerful Partnerships offers programs, as well as ideas, techniques, and models to help create successful law enforcement-refugee partnerships in your community. The programs were chosen from across the nation because they demonstrated innovation, replicability, collaborative nature,

The profiles of programs in Powerful Partnerships go beyond simply describing program activities to highlight techniques and strategies that can be broadly applied. They:

Work with law enforcement

Work with refugees

Involve young people

Involve parents and family

Target the needs of the community

Locate and use resources effectively

Help youth develop skills to help themselves

Develop and sustain culturally diverse partnerships

law enforcement involvement, relevance, results, and sustainability, as well as geographic, demographic, situational, and topical diversity.

The programs selected address problems that range from keeping youth in school and overcoming barriers between authorities and refugees to improving family communication and helping youth stay out of gangs. They also display diversity in program size, problem-solving approaches, budget requirements, length of operation, and program complexity. All 20 of the programs have the strong support of their communities, especially law enforcement; some were initiated by police.

These programs can be adapted to successfully address problems faced by communities across the nation, especially communities needing to overcome barriers, fear, and mistrust. Well-structured programs based on the lessons from these partnerships can produce exciting results that

- Decrease crime and violence;
- Decrease home invasions;
- Decrease the numbers of youths joining gangs;
- Increase reporting of crimes, including domestic violence;
- Increase refugee participation in civic activity;
- Increase self-esteem of refugee children, resulting in improved school attendance and performance;
- Increase the number of parents obtaining assistance for parenting issues, family violence, intergenerational conflict, and other personal obstacles to successful resettlement;
- Increase the feeling of safety in the community.

Powerful Partnerships is designed to be as useful as possible to a wide range of individuals in communities that differ in many respects. Knowing that it would be infeasible to develop a truly comprehensive list of programs, NCPC selected the programs highlighted in this book to provide a diverse sample of the many good programs in action today. Please note that, although these programs are accurately presented to the best of our knowledge, NCPC has not independently field-verified them; inclusion should not be construed as endorsement.

How To Use *Powerful Partnerships*

This document has been designed to help you understand key aspects of the problems and programs that address these problems; learn about effective programs through profiles; and identify a variety of resources that can help. Section 1 explains the need for forming collaborative partnerships between law enforcement and newly arrived Americans. It examines some stereotypes commonly held by both refugees and law enforcement officers; gives advice on how to choose community partners;

Tips From Police to Police on Partnering With Refugees

- Developing relationships with refugees is a long-term strategy, not a short-term project.
- Be flexible and creative. Traditional methods won't always work by themselves.
- Build trust. It will take time and patience to become accepted in a community.

From the beginning:

- Go into the community. Shop in local grocery stores, attend religious services and celebrations, and take part in community meetings.
- Use social events, such as block parties or holiday celebrations, as a time to begin relationships and conversations about community needs.
- Learn about the history of the people.
  - Where do they come from?
  - How did they get here?
  - Why did they come?
  - How long have they been here?
- Recruit and hire male and female ethnic officers to serve as liaisons.
- Think of refugees as potential productive community members who can make a difference.
- Identify the "players." Seek out people who are informal leaders in the community, as well as the formal leaders. Find out the key issues and opinions of all leaders and groups, before you bring them together for a meeting. Then, be prepared for various representatives to have totally different agendas.
- Be prepared for refugees to be suffering from culture shock. Parents experiencing change may hold on to their culture for some stability. They may feel uncomfortable with the freedom and liberty in the United States. For example, most American parents want their children to be independent. Many refugees may see this independence as lack of respect.
- Demystify law enforcement as much as possible. When appropriate, keep the community advised and up to date regarding an investigation's progress, techniques, and procedures.

lays out steps in developing partnerships; and provides lessons learned from some established programs and common characteristics of successful programs. It also provides some ideas to get started.

Section 2 is the heart of the book — the 20 successful partnership programs. These profiles of top-quality partnership programs convey strategies for developing similar programs in your community. Each profile examines the program's structure, staffing, activities, partners, and resources. It also addresses some of the challenges these programs encountered and how those were resolved. Contact information is provided for each program. The organizations that operate the 20 programs have kindly agreed to offer what help they can, but please understand that their resources, like yours, are limited.

Section 3 provides an extensive list of resources to help you develop, improve, and sustain your program. This section includes audio-visual and written materials and lists of resource organizations, agencies, and Internet resources.

We intend to continue to make information available about new and different strategies in refugee crime prevention. Use the tear-out card in the middle of the book to indicate that you have a successful refugee crime prevention strategy. Mail the card to National Crime Prevention Council, Attn: ONA, 1700 K Street, NW, Second Floor, Washington, DC 20006.

Can Refugees and Law Enforcement Work Together?

"What's Wrong With Those Police Officers?"

You have probably heard the negative stereotypes about law enforcement officers. "They are rude, arrogant, and loud. If you call them for help, they arrive at your house with lights flashing and radios blaring."

The perception of some refugees is that police arrive on the scene as the enforcer and quickly tell civilians what to do. They often act irritated, don't ask for residents' opinions, and admit that they can't do anything to help the victim. Refugees may even ask themselves, "What's wrong with those police? Can't they help us?"

What's the reality? Police officers are often called upon to act quickly to secure the crime scene area and protect the residents. "Twenty-four hours a day, seven days a week, 365 days a year, you have to be ready for what's around the next corner," explains Sgt. Judy Anderson of the Washington, DC, police department. The following scenarios may all happen to a police officer in the course of one day.

You're on patrol. A young man comes running out of a convenience store excitedly, maybe angrily. He's waving something. Is it a gun, a knife, or a loaf of bread? You can't tell. You can't stop to think. You have to act.

You get a call on a domestic disturbance. When you get there, the husband and wife are shouting at each other in a language you don't understand. The children are crying and the neighbors are crowded around. No one speaks a language you know but you have to act.

You stop by the neighborhood recreation center's after-school program. The kids know you. You help a child with her homework, but she seems distracted. She tells you her younger brother, who just started school, is being bullied. She cries because she went through the same thing. Her family is foreign, and the other kids just don't understand. You sympathize and try to help her figure out what to do.

More than 56,000 law enforcement officers were assaulted and 74 killed in 1995 alone, according to the Bureau of Justice Statistics. Police officers know the real dangers of their job. They realize that most people want to be helpful, but hesitation in acting can often mean the difference between life and death.

Most law enforcement and public safety officers joined their profession because they want to make a difference. They want to help make the system work to serve everyone fairly and to make their communities safer. But the job is not always a popular one. Sometimes they find that not only criminals, but even the general public, seem to have negative attitudes toward law enforcement.

"What's Wrong With Those Refugees?"

Refugees as well as law enforcement officers are easily stereotyped. You might hear, "Refugees don't want to work. They come here to use our welfare services." Or, "If they don't like the way things are, why don't they go back to where they came from?"

Some people think that refugees who live in the United States are not capable of achieving in this society or that they are lazy. It's fine if they want to come to this country, people say, as long as they can support themselves, quickly learn our language, and become fully "Americanized." What's the reality? Many refugees have fled persecution, war, and trauma in their countries. For the most part, they cannot go home. Some family members survived; some didn't. What situations do many refugee families face?

You sit in a public housing development, surrounded by crime, and remember the old days. You were a respected lawyer, or a successful farmer, or worked with humanitarian aid organizations, or fought side by side with Americans. Things weren't perfect, but you felt safe, your family was together, you had enough to eat, and you had a place to call home. You had support from your relatives and you shared a common language and culture.

But that was before there was war. During the war, your country was ravaged. Many people had to abandon their homes or their homes were burned. There was nothing to eat; you and your family were starving. There were explosions, fires, and men in uniform shooting at you and your family. You ran for your lives; your family was scattered.

Now you are resettled in a city where no one speaks your language and things are very different from your previous life. You dress differently than others and people stare at you. The children in school tease and bully your children. You are embarrassed to ask others to help you figure out how things work. And there is no one to turn to with these confusing new problems.

Most refugees worked hard and were self-supporting in their native countries. They have often overcome many hardships just to survive. But in the United States they are faced with trying to find a job without knowing the language while unable to go to school to learn English because they're looking for a job. Often refugee children learn English more quickly than adults and therefore control the communication with the rest of the world. Many adults feel they have lost control of everything in their lives.

And they feel there is no one they trust to help with these problems. Law enforcement officers in many countries are not trained to help the public as they are in the United States. In some countries police are even fearsome and cruel. Reaching out to law enforcement is not an alternative that most refugees would consider.

Yet these two groups — law enforcement and refugees — can and do work together effectively to make the community safer for all. A good first place to begin is to look at what the groups have in common.

What Do Refugees and Law Enforcement Have in Common?

It's easy to see the striking *differences* between refugees and law enforcement officers. But by looking past the obvious, you will find many similarities.

Both refugees and law enforcement need and want

- Safe communities for themselves and their children;
- The freedom to express values and religious beliefs;
- More youth staying in school and engaging in positive school activities;
- Fewer youth joining gangs and participating in disruptive, damaging activities;
- Employment that meets their families' financial needs;
- Safe, clean, affordable housing;
- Quality education;
- Healthy families;
- Respect; and
- Understanding of unique cultures and history and their influence on actions and perceptions.

In fact, a desire for a good quality of life unites us all. Common needs and wants mean common goals. Individuals united by common goals become more powerful when they join together to achieve those goals. That realization is at the heart of successful partnerships.

When a community's goals are safety and security, community members have a common interest with law enforcement officers and can most easily and effectively achieve their goals through crime prevention partnerships. These partnerships can include all kinds of community members; in fact any individual or organization in your community can be a valuable member of your coalition. You'll find that many of them will want to join your effort because they understand that everyone benefits from a safer, more peaceful community. Choosing a wide range of partners can help ensure your success.

Tips From Refugees to Refugees on Partnering With Law Enforcement

- Police in the United States are trained to uphold the public trust and to ensure the safety of all residents. They are available to help you with neighborhood disputes, and racial and ethnic problems, even if a crime hasn't been committed.
- Build a partnership with police focused on solving problems instead of reacting to crises.
- If you plan to involve law enforcement in a program or activity, include them during the planning stages. They will be more invested in a project they helped design.
- Act first in forming relationships with law enforcement, don't wait for others to make the first move.
    - Challenge law enforcement officers to compete in your favorite sport.
    - When you hold cultural activities, invite law enforcement. Send a letter and follow up in person. Consider giving law enforcement a few minutes to speak at your event.
- Establish a relationship with individuals you know you can call with problems, such as an officer in your precinct, or a liaison within your community.
- Develop a list of community members who can interpret for police, hospital, and other emergency personnel.
- Police are extraordinarily busy. If an officer does not seem interested in developing a partnership with you, talk to others in the department. Try someone in the department's community relations division. There are people in every department who want to work with the community; sometimes it's just a matter of finding the right one.
- Most police departments conduct limited training on other countries' cultures. Officers try to treat other cultures respectfully, but they make mistakes. And, since many officers haven't had much first-hand experience with other cultures, they can get easily frustrated. Try to be patient and work to educate officers who don't seem to understand your point of view.
- Police officers are paid to apprehend and prosecute criminals and cannot accept special gifts or rewards from victims.
- Remember that police officers do not investigate issues involving citizenship, immigration status, or deportation.

Building a Successful Crime Prevention Program

The Many Benefits of Collaboration

Increases the number of resources available

Broadens funding options

Distributes tasks more evenly

Broadens community support

Widens sphere of influence

Creates a broad base of partners and experience from which to draw

Lends credibility with a broader range of the community

Increases creativity by bringing more minds into the program

Choosing Your Partners in Crime Prevention

Partnerships are a powerful crime prevention tool. With several partners contributing to an effort, it can be more effective, farther reaching, and more comprehensive. Police officers who get information about crime from community members are able to perform their duties more effectively. As the representatives of local authority with the most access to the community, law enforcement officers can help refugee community members feel safe and welcome in their new homes. By communicating regularly, service providers of all kinds can offer appropriate, cost-effective, and comprehensive services, helping refugees to overcome their isolation and fear. Schools can work with social services, law enforcement, and parents to make sure that youth are encouraged and supported so they will stay in school. All make important contributions to the partnership.

- A key step in starting a partnership is for the law enforcement and the refugee communities to make contact; then they can move to discussing the problems the community is facing and what each can contribute to strategies and solutions.
  - **Police** gain respect and are able to accomplish more when they work in active partnership with refugees. "When people trust and believe in you, they'll support you," says Captain Andrew Hall of the Westminster, CA, Police Department. In such communities as Davenport, IA, (page 26) and Philadelphia (page 60), where refugees are comfortable communicating with law enforcement, they have been able to provide useful information to help solve and prevent crimes.
  - **Refugees** gain expertise and a better chance to succeed in their new country when they support law enforcement officials. A ten-year-old gang member in Phoenix (page 39) left the gang and started showing interest in positive activities after participating in an after-school program and developing a trusting relationship with a police officer. In Minneapolis, (page 33) parents and refugee community leaders are getting to know law enforcement and learning how to help their children, as well as adapting to the laws and practices in this country.

- The second step is to team with additional partners who have a stake in making the community a safer place to live. There are many possibilities for collaborative partners open to you. Here are just a few.

Local Decision Makers—Local officials have great interest in maintaining community safety, since people often view them as responsible for a community's quality of life. The mayor, the city council, and even state legislators can make powerful crime prevention partners. In Providence, RI, the mayor's office initiated a successful refugee youth program (page 118); in Salt Lake City, UT, a state senator plays an important role in the support and success of a neighborhood youth center.

Family Members—Youth program staff throughout the country emphasize the importance of involving the whole family in youth and community projects. From the Chief of Police in Elgin, IL (page 68), to the youth program director in La Crosse, WI (page 108), all say that family involvement is essential to success. The families working with these projects are equally enthusiastic, saying that being involved helps them stay in touch with what their children are doing. Family members can participate in program activities, volunteer for large special events, get involved in an ethnic PTA (page 33), or teach language, and ethnic dance or cooking.

Public Health Specialists—Crime prevention is a health issue; health professionals see first hand the injuries that are the results of violence. Doctors, nurses, hospitals, and clinics can all work with you to increase your program's effectiveness. Professionals can donate their services to families or work closely with law enforcement to provide training and identify community problems, as in Dallas (page 103). Hospitals can provide funding or facilities, or, as in Phoenix (page 39), community service project ideas for youth service projects.

Mental Health and Victim Assistance Professionals—Refugees are often suffering emotionally from their traumatic experiences. Professionals know that such traumas, left untreated, can have a negative effect on adjustment to this country, as well as long-term physical health. Mental health professionals can provide services for victims or perpetrators of domestic violence, as in Seattle (page 113) or time and expertise for traumatized children in such programs as the therapeutic summer camp in Miami (page 64).

Religious Leaders and Organizations—As one of society's powerful guiding forces, religious leaders can serve as a strong influence and lead the way for the rest of the community toward involvement in crime prevention. They can help start a program, as in New Orleans, LA (page 54), or they can provide support, such as facilities, space, and volunteers. In Lincoln, NE, the Interfaith Council's collaborative effort resulted in the creation of the Asian Community and Cultural Center, which includes a police storefront and other gang and crime prevention programs and services.

School Staff—Because education is a key not only to job skills but to acculturation, schools are often a key collaborative partner. They can provide facilities, staff, and ideas, as well as collaborate for funding. Schools also face significant crime and drug problems that partners can help with. The successful gang resistance program in Providence, RI (page 118), works with all the city's middle schools. And in Boston, MA (page 49), a high school was a founding partner in the coalition formed to help Somali youth.

Universities and Colleges—Understanding that they are an invaluable resource for the communities they belong to, universities, colleges, and community colleges are often among the most active partners. They can sponsor programs, such as the Youth Equestrian Program in Modesto, CA (page 77); their faculty can serve as advisors; research and other facilities are sometimes donated. Students can act as program development or research interns, or as youth mentors or tutors, as in Boston (page 49).

Children/Youth—Young people can be strong allies and incredibly effective spokespersons. They are eager to put their energy and zeal to work to prevent crime and violence. An NCPC survey found that nine out of ten youth in this country want to do something about the violence in our society, but only three out of ten know of anything that they personally can do. Talk to children and youth who may be looking for a service project, like those in Clarkston, GA (page 91), or approach existing youth programs as potential partners.

Victims of Violence—Victims often want to help because they know what crime feels like first hand, and they want to make sure others don't experience the same horror. Work with domestic violence programs, sexual assault and rape crisis centers, and victim/witness services. Helping them ensure that their services are culturally sensitive strengthens your coalition while enhancing their services, as is the case in Clarkston, GA (page 44).

Social, Civic, and Fraternal Groups—Because civic activity and pride often go down as crime goes up, community leaders are eager to create safer neighborhoods. Reach out to such organizations as civic associations and local women's or men's clubs whose mission includes serving the community. The Lions Club in Willows, CA, for instance, has taken charge of graffiti removal in the community, and the coalition in Clarkston, GA (page 44), has found the Junior League to be an invaluable partner.

Businesses—When customers are afraid of the streets leading to a business or fear visiting the mall where a shop is located, businesses lose money. Both large and small business owners understand that building a crime-free community is simply good business. A youth center in Wausau, WI, had a new floor installed by a company whose president sits on its Board of Directors; the space for the center is donated by Kraft Foods. The John Hancock Insurance Company in Boston worked with police to establish a year-round employment program for at-risk youth.

Neighborhood Groups—Residents care about the safety and quality of their neighborhoods and will often band together to clean up, share skills, and develop community awareness of problems. Existing neighborhood associations could be interested in working with you, or you can form your own. Neighborhoods in Philadelphia formed several Refugee Town Watches (page 60). In Phoenix, the city has a department specifically created to coordinate and assist neighborhood efforts throughout the city (page 39).

Communities all over the country are forming coalitions to reduce crime and improve quality of life, and you can do the same. But once you have your team, how do you develop specific programs that work?

Steps to Successful Crime Prevention Program

Thousands of people around the country have designed creative, effective programs that help stop violence in their neighborhoods and communities. This is a collaborative process from beginning to end. Start by convening a core group of individuals and organizational representatives who will benefit from the project's success. To ensure this meeting's effectiveness, you will need to provide translation services and to allow time for it in your planning. Here are some of the additional steps in building your crime prevention partnership program.

1. Find your collaborative partners.

Talk with people in the community who have vision and ideas, show dedication to your goals, and will be comfortable on your team.

Collaboration is much more than having a group of organizations and individuals "allow" their names to be listed as endorsements to your crime prevention project. Your core of collaborative partners should have a firm commitment to investing the time and energy and to bringing in the resources needed to ensure the project's success. Political leaders are essential partners.

2. Assess your needs.

Before you start your program, make sure you have an accurate pic-

ture of what is needed and why, and what are priorities for every group. For example, you may think youth need recreational activities, when what they really want is help with their school work.

- Ask everyone who might benefit from your project, youth, parents, teachers, school counselors, police, and juvenile justice officials what concerns them. Be sure to include people on both sides of controversial issues. Getting all sides around the table in the initial planning stages will facilitate the kind of lasting change you want.
- Convene focus group meetings; sometimes people think better together.
- Let information gathered from these groups guide the development of the project.
- See page 49 for ideas from the needs assessment conducted before starting the Somali Youth Project in Boston.

3. Determine existing assets and resources.

What is already available to you locally that can help you get your project started and keep it going?

- Your local park is a resource, as are the children in your neighborhood, and the convenience store on the corner. Think creatively!
- The refugee community is a resource; Lao PTA in Minneapolis (page 33) conducts cooking classes to teach others how to cook Lao food, and youth in New Orleans (page 54) perform dragon dances for a fee to raise money. In addition, refugee resettlement agencies and other service providers may have existing programs that can be expanded.
- Police are a resource. They bring tremendous knowledge about the legal system, understanding of local needs, ideas about improving the community, and access to government.
- Don't forget all the civic, religious, and educational organizations in your community that can provide resources, as well as act as partners.
- Look at the "Resources" part of each Successful Partnership Program in Section 2 of this book for many innovative ideas.

4. Develop an action plan.

Begin working with your collaborative partners to develop a plan of action to achieve your stated goal.

- Don't forget to include short-term as well as long-term accomplishments—small goals as well as large ones. Being able to show results quickly will assist you in developing community support from the very beginning.
- Be sure to include members of your target population as partners. To discuss the needs and strategies for a youth program, for example, you would include some youth.

Getting Community Resources

Answering these questions will help you and your partners plan and carry out your resource development strategy.

"Why are we here?"

"What do we want to do?"

"What do we have?"

"What do we need?"

"What are we going to use it for?"

"Who has what we need?"

"How will they benefit?"

"How do we get to know them?"

"How are we going to tell them our story?"

"What exactly needs to be done?"

"Which of us will take which of the tasks?"

"When will each task get done?"

- Never leave a meeting without specific commitments on the part of all participants.
- Detail steps to be taken and individuals to report progress at the next meeting.
- Establish the need and mechanism for communication between meetings.
- Set the date and agree on major agenda items for the next meeting.
- Your plan should include:
  - Resources, non-monetary as well as monetary.
    In-kind donations can comprise as much as 70 percent of your budget and save you a great deal of money. And don't forget that people are your best resources!
  - Evaluation (with measurable results).
    Proving that your project has a positive impact on the community will help you when you are looking for funding and other support. Ask yourself, "What do we mean by success? What will be different because of our work?"
  - Publicity and marketing.
    The more people who know what wonderful things you are doing, the more community support you have. Use the information about your impact and results from your evaluation to tell your story.
  - Plan B.
    Your group should prepare for things to happen differently from the way you planned them. Ask yourselves, "What can go wrong?" and then think ahead of time what you can do about it.
  - Celebration.
    Don't forget to plan for celebration of your accomplishments. Work it into your marketing and publicity for maximum impact.

Tips on building a successful program are helpful, but it's always best to learn from those who have been there. What are some of the similarities among the most successful programs? What problems did they encounter and how did they solve them? What have we learned from others?

What Have We Learned From Others?

Common Threads

Successful collaborative refugee crime prevention programs have a number of similarities. Being aware of these will help you design your programs for success.

Starting with the resources you have at hand, you can build a program whose success will help you obtain resources to expand and improve it.

- Don't reinvent the wheel. Find out who knows about similar programs in your community—or around the country. Existing programs can help you get started by providing materials, tips on lessons learned, further useful contacts, and other helpful advice.
- Start small. Focus on one specific need. Meeting that need successfully will give you credibility. The Dallas program (page 103) started with one officer and a case worker walking door to door in the refugee community. Later a police storefront was established and staffed by three Southeast Asian police liaisons. Now the storefront is staffed by eight officers and many civilian volunteers; has a bicycle unit; and operates a hotline, citizenship classes, neighborhood watches, and youth programs.
- Many of the programs in *Powerful Partnerships* started out entirely or largely volunteer-run. Volunteers can staff your program, develop and implement your evaluations, help plan and carry out your marketing strategy, work with the media, solicit funds and donations, and many other essential tasks.
- Getting started is half the battle; the other half is marketing your success.

Community problems are caused by a wide variety of factors, so it makes sense to use holistic approaches that attack problems from as many directions as possible. For instance:

- Instead of focusing a youth project on youth alone, involve the whole family.
- Partner with prosecutors, judges, probation officers, and victim assistance providers in addition to law enforcement officers.
- Involve mainstream community organizations, as well as refugees, in your work.
- Make sure that your plan provides for the celebration of short-term as well as long-term accomplishments.
- Constantly evaluate and promote your project's effectiveness and modify your plan as needed for improvement or to respond to changing circumstances.

Collaboration ensures that everyone benefits.

- To ensure that your community maintains its support of your project, let all the different groups involved take responsibility for the needs assessment, planning, resource development, implementation, and evaluation.
- The more support your program receives in-kind, the more money you will have for necessary cash outlays.
- By developing far-ranging community support of your program, you will expand future resources.

- By partnering with the media and publicizing your program well, you can gain support from the community as a whole. Develop a media handout that explains the accomplishments and benefits of your program. Keep an up-to-date media list.
- Develop several funding sources, so your program can survive the loss of any one.
- Remember local funding sources have a stake in your success and are often more likely to continue to support you than national ones. Encourage individual donations. More than 80 percent of funds are donated by individuals.

Lessons Learned

These words of wisdom, from those who have developed cross-cultural crime prevention programs, will help you avoid mistakes.

- Perseverance is the key to collaborative community crime prevention projects involving foreign-born residents and law enforcement.
- Language barriers make everything more difficult and time consuming, and cultural differences can create obstacles to your success.
- Perceptions of time differ greatly among cultures; in many cultures punctuality is not of great concern. The Georgia Coalition for Battered Refugee and Immigrant Women (page 44) resolved this difference by starting all meetings on time. This encouraged punctuality, as everyone was responsible for catching up on what they had missed.
- Social observances are more important in some cultures than others; it may be worth setting aside time at the beginning of every discussion to exchange brief social conversation before going on to business. Keeping this lesson in mind made working with the local refugee organizations much easier for the police in Westminster, CA.
- In some cultures, it's impolite to tell someone you didn't understand them. This can lead to serious miscommunication, but if all parties are aware of it, they can adjust their way of communicating and avoid problems. You can use newsprint for a visible recording of what is said or use feedback, having people repeat back they have heard. Or try sending handouts or agendas to participants ahead of time.
- Refugees and police alike benefit from finding out about potential challenges that may arise within the coalition, before they occur. Participants are more open to resolving communication problems if they've already discussed differences, similarities, and expectations. Sometimes this can be accomplished through diversity training, as with the Atlanta, GA, program (page 73).

One of the largest, most persistent problems faced by programs is difficulty in obtaining funding and other resources. Programs have learned that taking the time to tell their story is essential to successful resource development.

- Effective marketing doesn't just happen; you have to learn how to do it. Look around your own community for successful programs and ask them for tips and techniques.
- Planning your marketing strategy helps to ensure success. You might be able to find a college intern who specializes in marketing to help you plan.
- Make sure that your program evaluation focuses on impact. What does success look like? For instance, what is important is not the numbers of classes you provide, but what is different because people come to the classes.
- Get organized. Taking the time to organize your work pays off in the long run not only because you'll work more efficiently but also because others, such as volunteers, will be able to work with you more easily.
- Put everything into a database—your media contact list, your volunteers' duties and hours, your information about donors and funders—everything. The information is more flexible and accessible in a database.
- Keep track of what your volunteers do and how many hours they work. You can use this information to match other funding; you can show community support for your program. If youth involved in your program have a community service requirement for school, this information can help them get credit.
- Make sure that you, your staff, and volunteers always carry an up-to-date wish list of program needs so you can easily and effectively let people know. These needs can range from funds or space to office equipment or a vehicle. Organize a system for acknowledging donations quickly with a thank-you note and a receipt for tax deduction.

These lessons are helpful once you get started, but how do you do that? Where do you begin? Take a look at some ideas to get you started.

Ideas To Get You Started

For Refugees

Crime is everybody's problem. Get involved. The police need and want your help. Your cooperation and assistance will help them do their job more effectively! Remember, some of these tasks can be accomplished quickly, but some will take time and patience.

- Take a leadership role. Be a liaison for your community.
- Be your community's contact person for the police.
- Serve on a community advisory committee.
- Work with public agencies and neighborhood organizations. Don't be shy about letting them know who you are and what your community needs. They can also help you find out how the system works.
- Join a neighborhood clean-up. Involve everyone—teens, children, and senior citizens. Graffiti, litter, abandoned cars, and run-down buildings tell criminals that you don't care about where you live or about each other. Call the city public works department and ask for help in improving your neighborhood.
- Work with schools and PTAs to establish drug-free, gun-free zones and with recreation officials to do the same for parks.
- Involve the police in making sure all youth in the neighborhood have positive ways to spend their spare time through organized recreation, tutoring programs, part-time work, and volunteer opportunities.
- Work with police to set up a Neighborhood Watch or community patrol. Make sure your streets and homes are well lit.
- Form a Court Watch to help support victims and witnesses to see that criminals receive fair punishment.
- Ask police or local officials to use new ways to get criminals out of your building or neighborhood. Those might include enforcing anti-noise laws, housing codes, health and fire codes, anti-nuisance laws, and drug-free clauses in rental leases.
- Observe National Crime Prevention Month in October by holding rallies, marches, and other group activities to show you're determined to drive out crime and drugs.
- Develop and share a phone list of local organizations that can provide counseling, job training, guidance, and other services that neighbors might need.

For Law Enforcement

Your community is more diverse than you realize. Take advantage of all the different kinds of people to whom you have access by using their wide variety of strengths, their ideas, their energy, and their commitment to a safe and secure place to live. They will be pleased to work with you; they just may not know how to start.

- Review police reports on community crimes to learn about the current issues, trends, and concerns.

- Contact your local refugee resettlement agencies. The voluntary agencies (VOLAGs), Mutual Assistance Associations (MAAs), and other refugee service providers know about the needs as well as talents of the people they work with.
- Contact your State Refugee Coordinator, who can give you a picture of the demographics and needs of refugees around your state. Working closely with this person is often a key to success.
- Talk with your department's training unit about its diversity training component. Maybe they would like to work with refugees on developing a section to help officers understand and work collaboratively with ethnically diverse populations.
- Talk with your department's community relations unit about reaching out to refugees and immigrants. Newcomers need help in learning about the laws in this country.
- Consider starting a Citizens' Police Academy specifically for foreign-born residents. Remember when planning a special occasion, such as a Citizens' Academy or a recreational event, to hand out fliers that explain why it will be of interest (in various languages, if possible).
- Apply for funding designated to help refugees. These under-served and generally minority populations are sometimes eligible for special funding, which you might be able to tie into community crime prevention efforts. Be sure to involve refugee service providers and refugees themselves in planning programs.
- Work with community members to develop crime prevention stategies that fit their specific needs and issues; different communities have different problems.
- Respond to invitations from refugee groups for social events. Your appearance at community activities shows good will and interest that is a step toward building trust.
- Reply to invitations by extending your own—for example, by inviting refugee adults or youth on a ride-along. This could be their first chance to get an idea of what police in this country really do.
- Make the effort to collaborate as much as possible with appropriate agencies; they will share the responsibilities, so it won't all be up to you.

This list of starter ideas is not only for law enforcement; most community agencies and organizations will also find it useful for starting a partnership with the refugee community.

SECTION II

TWENTY SUCCESSFUL PARTNERSHIP PROGRAMS

Safe and Secure With WINGS

STRATEGY 1

We teach the community that they have a choice: 1) they can be afraid; 2) they can continue to be victimized by the gangs, or 3) in spite of fear of retaliation, they can stop the victimization by working with the police.

Corporal Brent Biggs
Davenport Police Department

Purpose

The need for the WINGS (Working in Neighborhoods to Gain Security) program became apparent in a community meeting in 1992 when Vietnamese and Bosnian refugees asked the Refugee Resettlement Program (RRP) for assistance in stopping a small local gang from terrorizing them. After two years of planning, the police chief introduced WINGS and a police officer to the refugee community. The goals of WINGS are to develop community crime prevention strategies that meet accepted police practice guidelines and are respectful of cultural differences. It also seeks to generate an interest among the refugee community in law enforcement as a career.

The officer began work by walking the neighborhoods with residents, visiting businesses and schools, and talking to people on the street. Soon, an ethnic community liaison was hired to work in partnership with the police officer, and together they got to know the neighborhoods and the residents. At meetings and informally, the officer and the liaison discussed home safety, personal safety, and other topics initiated by the community. With every contact, the bond of trust and respect between law enforcement and the refugee community was strengthened.

Program Structure

Staffing

- The program director of the RRP administers and coordinates the program.
- A police officer from the Davenport Police Department is assigned to work with the refugee community.
- An ethnic community liaison to the police works with the police officer, acting as a bridge between the refugee community members and law enforcement.
- Twelve regularly scheduled volunteers from the refugee community and additional volunteers as needed provide oral and written translation, arrange special events, and perform other tasks required for general program support.

Community Partners

Davenport Police Department

The Refugee Resettlement Program

The Friendly Vietnamese Association

Buddhist and Catholic leadership

Scott County Providers

The Iowa Department of Human Services/ Bureau of Refugee Services

Activities

The following services are provided in the refugee community by WINGS:

- Guest speakers address topical issues at quarterly community meetings and presentations concerning laws and safety issues.
- Victims of assault get some compensation.
- Refugees get assistance in the court system.
- Videos and translated handouts are distributed to provide information on such topics as the Miranda warning, what to do if stopped by a police officer, and domestic violence.
- The officer and the liaison participate in English as a Second Language (ESL) classes in four schools at least twice during the school year and the adult ESL programs at least once a year.
- WINGS acts as a resource for the schools, the Department of Human Services, the FBI, the fire department, and the Department of Corrections and responds to requests from many county agencies for services and presentations; and
- The police officer learned important phrases in Vietnamese to facilitate communication.

The police officer and liaison work together to

- Visit neighborhoods after school and on weekends to get to know the children, families, and local activities; to reinforce safety issues; and to reduce harassment;
- Develop and maintain Neighborhood Watch activities; and
- Attend community meetings and social events.

In addition, the community liaison performs such tasks as

- Patrolling in business areas;
- Being available to residents on a walk-in basis;
- Responding to requests for assistance from other law enforcement officers and agencies such as juvenile courts and Department of Human Services;
- Providing in-service training related to cultural awareness and gangs;
- Attending social events; and
- Teaching ethnic cultural guidelines to the police officer.

For police departments, the WINGS staff

- Holds diversity training workshops; and
- Presents the WINGS model to encourage the development of similar programs and to inform the law enforcement community about the advantages of involving refugees in crime prevention.

Getting the Community Involved

WINGS encouraged refugee community participation in its crime prevention program through the following actions:

- Program staff held open meetings with community leaders to provide information and to answer questions about the resettlement program's services; posted notices of meetings in public places and sent them home with school children; and called families at home to discuss the meetings, answer any questions, and learn about any concerns.
- The police officer passed out business cards in the community, explained who he was, what he did, and how he could be reached.
- Officers wore plain clothes when in the community because they found this helps the refugees be more relaxed and speak more freely.
- To gain police department support, WINGS staff met with police to explain the program and desired outcomes, they collected and provided information about crime and victimization in the refugee community to support the need for the program, and implemented a police diversity training program.
- A member of the community who spoke the refugees' language and came from the same culture was chosen to be the refugee community liaison.
- The chief of police provided support by introducing the police officer to the refugee community, assisting in the interview process for the community liaison, and asking the refugee community for ideas about how they thought WINGS could help them. Continued support by the chief encourages community involvement.
- WINGS is located in the RRP office. By arranging for refugees to contact the liaison at a familiar place instead of the police department, staff helped refugees become comfortable with the program.

Results

- Home invasions by local gangs stopped once the gang members' identities were made known to WINGS.
- Two drug houses were closed.
- One gang of seven to eight young men ceased terrorizing the refugee community after they were identified to WINGS.
- Charges were filed in four felony cases that had been closed as unsolved by the Davenport Police Department.
- An extortionist was arrested and sentenced in court using information provided in a community meeting.
- Reporting of criminal activity and suspicious behavior has increased, producing more recorded crimes as the community has become more comfortable with the police.
- Although the number of reported crimes went up, actual community crime problems decreased, and community members are reporting they feel safer now.
- Domestic violence victims are able to ensure that their abusers comply with court orders (usually to attend the batterer education program). They are also aware of their full legal rights and take advantage of available services.

Challenges Faced and Resolved

- There was a reluctance on the part of the refugee community, because of fear, cultural differences, and language barriers, to take a step beyond asking the Refugee Resettlement Program to stop the crime.

♦ The community liaison works closely with the community to familiarize the refugees with resources other than the RRP. The program now acts as a sub-office for other community service providers, especially law enforcement. This facilitates more comprehensive services for refugees.

- There were delays in the development of a partnership with the police department.
    - The lack of funds and staff at the police department prevented assigning an officer to the refugee community.
    - After funds were available, there was a delay in announcing the opening at the police department.
    - The delay in selecting the police officer caused a delay in the hiring of the liaison.
    - Some police officers had difficulty understanding the grant and its purpose.

♦ Diversity training allowed the police to fully understand the necessity of the WINGS project.

♦ Staff met several times with the police to explain the program.

- The Davenport Police Department was not aware of any problems within the refugee community that would be of concern to police.

♦ The refugee community and the RRP provided information to the police department concerning the problems the refugees were facing.

■ Other minority groups resented not having a similar project.	♦ The WINGS program expanded and now serves both Bosnian and Vietnamese refugees. ♦ WINGS is funded for refugee services only but will provide all possible assistance to any groups who desire and have obtained funding to start a similar program.
■ Language barriers existed for both the refugee community and the police department.	♦ Some police learned key Vietnamese words and phrases to reduce the language barrier. ♦ The liaison acts as a translator between the refugee community and the police department.

Resources and Support

- Funding for the community liaison and for the police officer's overtime is provided by a four-year grant from ORR through the Bureau of Refugee Services of Iowa.

Community partner contributions:

- The Refugee Resettlement Program, lead partner, provides office facilities, the program director, and administrative functions.
- Davenport, IA, Police Department authorizes overtime for the police officer and provides other necessary police resources to work with the project, including in-kind donations of a police vehicle and gasoline.
- The Friendly Vietnamese Association coordinates community meetings, prepares notices for the meetings, and facilitates telephone communication.
- Buddhist and Catholic leadership assist in coordinating community meetings.
- Scott County Providers (a group of agencies and service providers, such as school teachers, the Department of Human Services, the

Center for Alcohol and Drug Services, the Department of Health, as well as individuals and refugee community members) meet monthly to ensure the needs of the community are being met and problems are resolved or prevented.

- The program receives donations from churches and other private organizations.
- The Department of Human Services/Bureau of Refugee Services for the State of Iowa provides general support and expertise, including writing grant proposals.

Who To Contact

Nora J. Dvorak
WINGS (Working in Neighborhoods to Gain Safety)
Refugee Resettlement Office
1706 North Brady, Suite 208
Davenport, IA 52803
Phone: 319-324-7913
Fax: 319-383-5534

Lao PTA Pulls Children Off the Streets

STRATEGY 2

Ninety-eight percent of the children we serve stay in school and earn average grades or better.

Lao PTA
Program Director

Purpose

In 1992, 16 of the 43 youth murdered in Minneapolis, MN, were from the Near North neighborhood, where more than 40 percent of the population lived below the poverty level and many were unemployed. Juvenile delinquency rates for the Lao youth who lived there were increasing at an alarming rate as youth were being drawn to and affected by gang-related crime.

Parents, teachers, and the staff of Lao PTA began a Youth Crime Prevention and Intervention Program in 1993 in response to the growing concern for the safety and future of the Lao children. The main goal of the program is to provide productive activities and support groups for Lao youth.

Program Structure

Staffing

- An executive director manages the program and supervises many of the activities.
- A youth specialist handles administrative issues, plans the program, and works directly with youth and the school in the after-school programs.
- A youth outreach worker works directly with youth and assists in the after-school programs.
- There are five volunteer tutors.
- A parent coordinator conducts workshops for parents.
- Parent volunteers assist staff in teaching Lao history and culture.

Activities

Activities are designed to

- Improve English language skills;
- Improve academic performance;
- Encourage Lao children to stay in school; and
- Build self-esteem by teaching about heritage, culture, history, language, and traditional dances.

Community Partners

Lao PTA

Minneapolis Police Department

Minneapolis School System

Parks and recreation agencies

- Two-hour tutorials and study groups meet twice a week at schools, and the Lao PTA helps 215 children with language skills and homework.
- Supervised after-school recreational activities at six sites include
  - Individual and team sports for 100 girls and boys include ping pong, tennis, badminton, basketball, volleyball, soccer, and kator (a Lao game);
  - Computer skills classes for ninety students (once a week during the school year, twice a week during the summer);
  - Two peer support group sessions, each week, to improve decision making ability (ten girls meeting with a female facilitator and ten boys with a male facilitator);
  - Instruction in Lao traditional dance once a week for 70 elementary school children from a variety of ethnic groups;
  - Band practice, each week, for 30 children at the Lao PTA; and
  - Classes for 100 youth in Lao history, culture, language, cooking, music, and dance, once a week during the school year and twice a week during the summer;
- There are three cultural and social gatherings a year for 70 families to celebrate young people's achievements and to encourage the development of positive family relationships.
- The program conducts workshops for 80 parents on
  - the American juvenile justice system, appropriate means of discipline, and parenting skills;
  - the American system of education and parents' role in their children's education; and
  - recognizing the warning signs of gang involvement or substance abuse.

Results

- Some rival gang members became friends. Lao PTA recruited high-risk teens from different gangs to participate on their winning soccer team. Team loyalty replaced gang loyalty, and rival gang members bonded despite their differences.
- The Minneapolis Police Department reports that crime and violence within the Lao community has decreased.

- School officials report that many youth who were perceived as troublemakers and are now participants in the Lao PTA program have improved their school performance and behavior.
- School officials report that increased numbers of program participants are wearing more conventional clothing instead of gang apparel.
- Parents report they are satisfied with the results of the Lao PTA program. Their children are not associating with delinquent youth and are succeeding in school and the community.
- Lao youth report they feel better about themselves, their families, and school than they did one year ago.
- Staff members observe that participating youth handle conflicts and stressful situations more effectively.

How Your Program Can Serve as a Community Resource

Serving as a community resource benefited Lao PTA in several ways. After the mainstream community began to see refugees as an asset to their city, resources and collaboration increased. To create a positive image for your program, try these tips:

- Provide services for schools:
  - Keep lines of communication open between parents and school officials through frequent visits by the parent coordinator to the school,
  - Provide translation and interpretation services for parents at school conferences and meetings, and
  - Monitor Lao students' progress by keeping records of attendance and grades.
- Get involved with the police department:
  - Participate in regular meetings to exchange information on neighborhood issues and discuss how to deal with the crime and violence.
- Work with the MAAs, social services, and other mainstream agencies:
  - Collaborate with other community-based organizations to provide cultural and sports activities for the children and youth, and
  - Encourage youth from diverse cultures to participate in sports together to ease tensions and to increase respect and trust among youth of different ethnic groups.

- More than 50 percent of participating youth are able to perform at least one traditional Lao dance. Fifty students in the Lao PTA's Super Teen Artists Group are invited to dance for audiences across Minnesota.
- Recognizing the program to be effective and appropriate in meeting the needs of the Lao community, state officials now provide financial support.

Challenges Faced and Resolved

■ Attracting gang members to the program proved difficult.	♦ Peers and parents were persistent in their outreach. They told gang members about the program, handed out fliers describing the program, and made sure that gang members knew about the advantages program participants enjoy, such as uniforms, equipment, and a safe place to play the sports.
■ The location made transportation a problem because the Lao PTA building is located in one of the more dangerous neighborhoods in Minneapolis.	♦ The program acquired a 15-seat van, which, along with staff cars, is used to transport youth to and from the premises. ♦ School buses are used for some after-school activities. ♦ Staff plan to acquire a second van in the spring of 1998.
■ There is a high demand for participation in the program but a small staff to provide services.	♦ Lao PTA staff work many extra hours to meet program needs. ♦ Community volunteers supplement staff efforts.
■ Another obstacle was the lack of space to adequately provide services to refugee children and their families.	♦ Use of the city parks and gymnasiums to practice soccer and other sports alleviates the space problem

- In the near future, the Lao will no longer be eligible for refugee funding, and grants from foundations are very competitive.

♦ Lao PTA staff continue to work very hard to gain trust from both the community and funders by providing services that meet the needs of the community and by providing proof of program successes to potential funders.

Resources and Support

- Funding for three full-time staff is provided by:
  - Multiple-year grants from a few key national and local foundations and corporations, and
  - Small donations from churches and civic groups.
- Volunteers, including five volunteer tutors, donate hundreds of hours to help staff run the program.
- There is state support for three programs: crime prevention, chemical dependency prevention, and the after-school program.
- The Lao dance troupe, Super-Teen Artists, donates some of the income they earn back to the Lao PTA.

Community partner contributions:

- The Lao PTA, lead partner, provides staffing, volunteer coordination, and facilities.
- The Minneapolis Police Department (MPD) conducts workshops for parents and youth and participates in regular PTA meetings to exchange information and solve problems. The MPD also holds an annual soccer game and picnic for youth in the area.
- The Minneapolis School System provides buses and facilities for tutoring and recreational activities.
- Parks and recreation agencies make space available for sports and cultural activities at several parks, fields, and gymnasiums throughout the city.

Who To Contact

Mr. Khao Insixiengmay
Lao Parents and Teachers Association
430 Bryant Avenue North
Minneapolis, MN 55405
Phone: 612-374-2447
Fax: 612-374-5997

Lao PTA's Super Teen Artists performing Lao modern folk dance "Lee-Tan Don" at the First Annual Lao Youth Celebration in 1996.

Replacing Guns With Good Clean Fun

STRATEGY 3

Super Saturday has helped me realize that I can do good things for others and have a lot of fun instead of joining a gang or using drugs.

A fifth grade program participant

Purpose

Almost all of the Mountain View Elementary school students are from low-income families and many are refugee children. Drugs, violence, and gang activity are common. To engage these vulnerable children in positive attitudes and to build bonds between students and police, the Phoenix Police Department initiated a collaborative project providing wholesome, educational, and entertaining activities. The Super Saturdays Program began when the police department received a grant from the governor's office in 1997.

Program Structure

Staffing

- Officers with patrol duty in the Mountain View School area plan and lead activities.
- Hospital staff, teachers, police officers, fire and human services department personnel, and adults and teenagers within the community donate time and materials.

Activities

- Youth service projects, such as
  - Hand painting special event tablecloths for the hospital,
  - Cleaning up a half-mile strip of road leading to the school,
  - Creating a garden around the school, and
  - Planting shade trees on the school grounds;
- A bicycle rodeo, during which youth from a Police Explorer Post guided the participants through the rodeo course and graded them for safety certification;
- Fix Your Bike Day, when police gave away 78 bicycles they helped children repair;
- It's Your Health Day, with activities teaching the importance of eating properly, staying healthy, and avoiding drugs;
- Safety Day, teaching fire safety, personal safety, and home security;
- Basketball and soccer clinics organized by volunteer high school students; and
- A Harvest Festival.

Community Partners

Phoenix Police Department

Mountain View School

John C. Lincoln Hospital

Results

- The Super Saturdays Program helps kids stay out of gangs by
  - Attracting them to positive and worthwhile activities free from drugs, violence, and gang activity. One ten-year-old gang member left his gang after making posters for school activities and developing a positive relationship with a police officer. Participating children have become engaged in positive alternatives to crime and value the program.
  - Guiding children's outlook to become less self-centered through service projects for others.
  - Barring gang attire, colors, or signs during activities.
- Children are more comfortable with law enforcement officers because police participate in activities and become familiar faces.
- Almost 150 children have benefited directly. Program evaluation results show that they not only feel more comfortable with the police, but they have also raised their grades and improved their behavior in school.

Challenges Faced and Resolved

- The proposed budget called for approximately $25,000, but only $6,100 was raised, so some activities were limited.

♦ The program continued on a reduced scale by recruiting more volunteers, increasing in-kind contributions of employee time from the three partnering agencies, and obtaining community contributions.

- Teachers are too busy to arrange extra daily activities for the students. Planning activities was primarily the responsibility of the police officers.

♦ In the future, a planning committee, consisting of police officers, teachers, and children will help plan all Super Saturday activities. It is important to include children in the planning process. In this program, the children suggested one of the more successful service projects, planting trees.

- At the beginning of the program, there were concerns about the use of the school for the Saturday activities. The principal of the school was reluctant to entrust a teacher with the key, because he was concerned with safety and school security. The first Saturday there was no one to let participants into the building, despite an arrangement the principal made with a janitor.

- ♦ After seeing the close supervision of the students by police officers and teachers and witnessing the positive effects the program had on the children, the principal agreed to provide a key.

Refugee children learn from police how to fix bicycles on Fix Your Bike Day.

Bikes and Skills For Needy Children

Here's what happened during Phoenix's Fix Your Bike Day Program.

- The first Saturday
  - Police taught bicycle safety laws and used videos to illustrate safe behavior on bicycles and what to do in an accident.
  - Everyone participated in a bicycle rodeo.
- The next Saturday, police conducted Fix Your Bike Day.
  - Police officers brought 78 bicycles that had been abandoned and impounded.
  - Teachers identified children who were behaving and doing well with their schoolwork, and those children chose which of the 78 bicycles they wanted to repair. Other children were allowed to work on any of the remaining bikes. (Children who already owned bicycles could also bring them to repair.)
  - The police officers helped children repair their bikes by providing spare bicycle parts and teaching them repair techniques.
  - After the bicycles were repaired, the children got to keep the ones they had fixed.
  - The hospital and a water company donated beverages, and a thrift bakery provided snacks for the police and children.

- It was important to get to know students and their needs.

♦ Teacher participation is essential to making the program a success. The teachers in the program already know the students, which makes it easier for the officer to maintain control and to run the activities effectively. Teachers also complement the police officers with their knowledge of how to keep children's attention.

Resources and Support

- Grant funding is provided by the Division of Drug Policy of the Governor's office.
- Volunteers from the community provide supplies, transportation, and many volunteer hours. For instance, in addition to high school youth helping with the sports clinics, a volunteer from a local insurance agency etched identity numbers onto the bicycles; a representative from the gas company brought a backhoe and assisted with planting the trees; a high school ROTC drill team performed, made a presentation about its program, and stayed to interact with the children; and activities were supervised by staff from the hospital, police, and school, as well as parents and community volunteers.

Community partner contributions:

- Phoenix Police Department serves as lead partner, with police officers planning and conducting activities for the children.
- Mountain View School provides space and referrals for the program.
- John C. Lincoln Hospital provides children with snacks and opportunities for service projects and training sessions.

Who To Contact

Lieutenant Warren Taylor
Phoenix Police Department
16030 North 56 Street
Phoenix, AZ 85254
Phone: 602-495-5006
Fax: 602-495-3639

Joining Forces Against Domestic Violence

STRATEGY 4

I am very glad I found a place where I can make connections into American life.

A shelter resident

Purpose

Domestic violence can be devastating. Imagine being brutalized by a family member and then seeking help from a series of agencies that are not working together. Your refugee or immigrant service doesn't know anything about domestic violence. You find a domestic violence shelter but, when you arrive, staff and programs are not equipped to deal with your problems, your language, or your culture.

That was the situation in Atlanta until 1994 when five ethnic agencies—the Center for Pan-Asian Community Services; Jewish Family and Career Services; Mercy Mobile's Latino Families at Risk Program; Raksha, Inc., for South Asians in Distress; and the Refugee Family Violence Prevention Project—formed an alliance to combat domestic violence.

This alliance, the Georgia Coalition for Battered Refugee and Immigrant Women, is dedicated to ending family violence against women, children, and the elderly in refugee and immigrant communities by providing culturally diverse and culturally sensitive services.

Program Structure

Staffing

The Coalition does not have any paid staff. The following volunteers from the five coalition agencies donate their time to ensure the smooth operation of the coalition:

- Ten bilingual/bicultural caseworkers,
- One employment specialist, and
- One volunteer coordinator facilitates the work of the five agencies.

Activities

The coalition

- Developed the International Women's House (IWH), a shelter for battered immigrant and refugee women. The coalition oversees the shelter, safety planning, legal advocacy in courts for domestic violence cases, counseling, translation and interpreting, immigration referrals, ESL services, and life skills training.
- Developed a chart, "Police Response to Domestic Violence in Ethnic Communities," to assist police in handling ethnic domestic violence effectively.

Being in a coalition is like being in a marriage. Just because you have agreed to be together and work toward the same goal does not mean that you will have to think and behave the same. You are a family and should accept that there will be differences.

D. BryAnn Chen
Coalition Coordinator

- Developed a domestic violence services wallet card in five languages for police use.
- Conducted a workshop on diversity and domestic violence awareness in ethnic communities for the Georgia Commission for Family Violence.
- Conducted training for Olympic Crisis Response Team in 1996.
- Is developing a national support network for battered refugee women.
- Is making mainstream battered women's services more accessible to refugee women by conducting dozens of training sessions per year. Training topics on domestic violence and refugees include
  - Domestic violence and its roots
  - Domestic violence as a barrier to self-sufficiency for refugees
  - Domestic violence as a hindrance to service provision for refugees
  - Effective educational strategies and materials for refugee communities

  Training topics for mainstream service providers include
  - Providing culturally appropriate services to refugee women and children
  - Using community resources to assist refugees
  - Making mainstream services more accessible to refugees
  - Preparing for the results of effective outreach (increased numbers of refugee women and children needing specialized services)

Results

- In May 1997, the coalition opened a two-bedroom shelter for battered refugee and immigrant women; seven refugee women were housed in the first nine months.
- The coalition was able to increase the options available to women served by its member agencies.
- Coalition agencies have seen an increased understanding of the issue of domestic violence among the women they serve. They now take action to become self-sufficient and free from violence in their homes.

- Mainstream agencies in surrounding counties are providing more culturally sensitive services to battered refugee and immigrant women.
- Police report that the chart "Police Response to Domestic Violence in Ethnic Communities" is very useful, and officers in several counties are using the five-language wallet card.
- Coalition members have observed an increase in police requests for assistance in handling domestic violence cases in refugee and immigrant communities.

Challenges Faced and Resolved

It was difficult for all agencies involved to work together effectively in the beginning.

- There was miscommunication and misunderstanding among various coalition members.
  - ♦ The coalition obtained mediation services from someone with ties to the parties involved but not a coalition member.
- There was misunderstanding and confusion about the roles each agency was to play.
  - ♦ The ethnic agencies learned to communicate their needs in a clear and direct way. The American-born partners began to participate in the meetings held by the ethnic agencies. Both groups put their opinions, requests, and needs in writing.
- The various agencies had differing abilities.
  - ♦ The group discussed the different abilities of each agency and agreed on a balance of responsibilities.
- There was confusion about goals, objectives, and definitions; the agencies defined domestic violence differently.
  - ♦ Coalition members met periodically to define their goals and objectives and to define the terms they were using.

Community Partners

Refugee Family Violence Prevention Project

Center for Pan-Asian Community Services

Shalom Bayit, Jewish Family and Career Services

Mercy Mobile's Latino Families at Risk Program

Raksha, Inc., for South Asians in Distress

- There wasa lack of communication between the Junior League and the coalition regarding the decisions made about the IWH. Each group was making decisions without knowing what the other group was doing.

♦ The director of the IWH now acts as liaison between the two groups, relaying the minutes of each group's meetings to the participating agencies.

- Some people were often late because time values differ from culture to culture.

♦ Instead of waiting for everyone to arrive, meetings started promptly; the latecomers had to rely on minutes for information they missed. This encouraged punctuality.

Creating a Powerful Multiethnic Coalition Against Family Violence

- Convene a meeting with representatives from all agencies that work with domestic violence and those that work with refugees. Develop a shared vision.
- Assess the needs of the community.
- Turn your vision into goals and a mission statement.
- Define responsibilities and duties of each member group.
- Approach a variety of agencies for support. Don't exclude mainstream organizations. For example, the coalition has found the Junior League to be extremely supportive and helpful.
- Begin educating the refugee and mainstream communities about the problems.
- Begin the process of recruiting and hiring staff. You'll need to have someone who can focus full time on this project.
- Recruit volunteers.
- Work with the media to educate the community and to publicize your efforts.
- Ensure that all refugee and immigrant agencies are working together.

Resources and Support

- Each of the five organizations in the coalition has support from many community-based organizations, local corporations, and individuals.
- Funding for the shelter and community outreach activities is provided by the Atlanta Women's Fund and other local foundations and individuals, the Criminal Justice Department, the Office of Housing and Urban Development, and ORR.
- The Georgia State Refugee Coordinator assists in making mainstream program services accessible.
- DeKalb County Board of Health assists in training workshops for public health centers.
- Individuals from the Chinese community assist in transportation, ESL, office work, and general city survival education.
- Students from local colleges help with coordinating research and compiling informative manuals concerning the IWH and the coalition.

Who To Contact

Arek Strzelecki
Refugee Family Violence Prevention Project
Newcomers' Network, Inc.
3647 Market Street
Clarkston, GA 30021
Phone: 404-299-6265
Fax: 404-299-6218

Off the Streets and Out of Trouble

STRATEGY 5

The students I referred [to the program] have shown a marked improvement both in conduct and in effort.

A teacher at English High School

Purpose

In Boston, MA, Somali parents knew their children were at risk for drug use, violence, and dropping out of school. What they didn't know was how to contact the schools to find out what problems their children were facing or what types of discipline they were allowed to use to correct their children's behavior.

In December 1996, the International Rescue Committee partnered with English High School, the Boston Public Health Department's Immigration and Refugee Office, and the Somali Development Center to begin the Somali Youth Program. The purpose was to

- Help students develop
  - The ability to communicate effectively and appropriately in English;
  - An understanding of American culture;
  - Knowledge and skills necessary to preserve their health and well-being;
  - Knowledge and skills necessary to be successful in the workplace; and
  - Basic skills through individual tutoring, group instruction, and homework help.
- Assist parents with strategies to help their children adjust to the new culture.

Program Structure

Staffing

- A full-time program director administers and coordinates the program.
- Three part-time teachers provide tutoring and instruction.
- Five volunteer teachers from universities provide tutoring and instruction.
- Volunteer teachers from the Somali community and the community at large provide tutoring and instruction.
- One part-time public health educator provides instruction and health counseling.

- One part-time employment counselor maintains an employment database and provides job skills training.
- One part-time coach supervises athletic activities.

Activities

- During the school year, students spend two hours a day, four days a week, for 36 weeks, in classes. The program curriculum includes
  - ESL lessons incorporating nutrition, fitness, personal hygiene, coping with stress, violence prevention, reading, writing, listening, speaking, math, interpersonal communication methods, problem solving, planning, and decision making. The sessions introduce new vocabulary and skills tailored to the content of the lesson;
  - Individual tutoring and homework assistance during the first hour of the session;
  - Computer labs and instruction during the first hour of the after-school program at three locations; and
  - Computer math tutorial at the Somali Development Center.
- The program is flexible. The entire two hours can be used for special programs, field trips, or remedial help.
- Following the two-hour program, youth can participate in supervised recreational activities at the community center, which include individual and team sports, traditional dance, swimming, or craft workshops.
- The summer program at the Jamaica Plain Community Center is open to middle school and high school youth, from 9 a.m. to 3 p.m., five days a week, for six weeks. The program includes
  - Academic classes in the morning;
  - Sports, supervised by a paid coach with volunteers, including intramural and citywide basketball, soccer, and volleyball games for boys and girls;
  - Life skills program that includes dance, artistic expression, swimming, and cultural education on alternate days;
  - Fridays are "activities day" for special events, such as picnics or field trips to museums, the aquarium, and other places of interest.

Results

- This program has successfully helped those who were in danger of dropping out, using drugs, or delinquency. These youth have shown improvement in their behavior, academic performance, and social adjustment to life in the United States.
- When the program started, a number of the Somali youth at English High School were getting into trouble and getting arrested. Since the program began, none of the youth participating in the program have been arrested. In 1997, law enforcement officers commended the program for successfully keeping Somali youth off the streets and out of trouble for the entire summer.
- When the Somali Youth Program was created, Somali youth were fighting with Hispanic and African-American youths; these fights have diminished.
- The sports and recreational activities have been instrumental in stopping fights. The coach enforces, equally and without appeal, a three-day suspension for all parties involved in fighting. This has resulted in peer encouragement and enforcement.

A Thorough Needs Assessment Pays Off

The Somali Youth Program works because it's what the community wants and needs. To be sure the program would be successful, the coalition partners used focus groups and surveys to gain input from these groups:

- Teachers and school administrators;
- Students who might use the program,
- Students applying to the program,
- Parents,
- Community elders, and
- The public health department.

The information provided through these focus groups and surveys determined the curriculum. Now, to ensure program flexibility, staff continue to survey these and other concerned youth and adults for information about what's working and what should be changed. In this way the program maintains its effectiveness.

Community Partners

International Rescue Committee

Somali Development Center

Department of Public Health

English High School

- Some Somali high school students are providing volunteer peer mentoring and tutoring.
- The collaborative after-school program has been so successful that English High School initiated a similar one in February 1998, to provide services to a wider range of students. The Somali Youth Program now has the support of six more school teachers and use of additional school facilities, such as the library and computer room.

Challenges Faced and Resolved

- Parents did not trust the program.
  - ♦ Staff explained the program to parents, both at school and at home in one-on-one meetings. They explained that the program is consistent and reliable in its dealings with all children.
  - ♦ Parents were encouraged to get involved in the school so they would understand the benefits of the Somali Youth Project. Now, Somali parents are active in the PTA, as well as the after-school programs, where they serve as mentors and tutors and teach Somali crafts, dance, and language.
- Students didn't want to be in a high school classroom all day and then go to another classroom with an ESL teacher. Because of the structured and rigid nature of the program, only 16 youths signed up and their attendance was sporadic.
  - ♦ A new program director was hired who implemented educational and tutorial activities designed to be flexible and to accommodate the needs of the participants in the after-school program. A broader range of supervised activities for the after-school recreation program and the summer program were planned. After the new activities began, attendance skyrocketed. In fact, the program had to adjust to accommodate the larger number of students who wanted to participate.

Resources and Support

- Funding for three full-time staff and three part-time staff is provided by
  - a three-year grant from ORR,
  - the state Office for Refugees and Immigrants,
  - the Governor's Alliance Against Drugs, and
  - the Jamaica Plain Area Planning Action Council.
- Non-monetary contributions include in-kind administrative support from IRC and English High School, as well as volunteer teachers from two area universities, the Somali community, and the mainstream community.
- The coalition partners provide primary support as follows:
  - The International Rescue Committee provides administrative and financial services and program guidance, as well as space and office materials.
  - Somali Development Center provides volunteers, volunteer teachers, computer facilities, a math tutoring program, outreach, translation and interpreting, a database for youth services, employment counseling, and mentoring.
  - Department of Public Health provides materials, workshops, and a part-time public health educator who serves as a confidant for youth at the school.
  - English High School provides teachers, facilities, guidance counselors, and academic assessment and review. Partnering with this school is essential to the success of the project.
- The Massachusetts Prevention Center provides workshops and information about drug education and prevention and violence prevention.

Who To Contact

Saida Abdi
International Rescue Committee
162 Boylston Street, Suite 50
Boston, MA 02116
Phone: 617-482-1154
Fax: 617-482-7922

Reversing the Trend Toward Youth Violence

STRATEGY 6

If this program didn't exist, I would be on the street smoking crack.

A youth program participant

Purpose

Since 1975, a large number of Vietnamese refugees have resettled in the Versailles Gardens community of New Orleans. Recently many of the youth have become involved in crime and drugs. To help these teens resist negative influences, the staff at the Catholic Charities Archdiocese of New Orleans began the Versailles Asian Youth Program (VAYP) in 1994.

The program targets at-risk youth in the Versailles Gardens community. Counselors try to reach youth before they get into serious trouble through activities that build their self-esteem and prepare them for the future.

Program Structure

Staffing

- A full-time youth coordinator serves as liaison between parents, youth, and the local church parish.
- Two full-time youth counselors work with youth and school officials.
- Volunteers from the church community provide general support for the program.

Activities

The program has a three-tiered structure:

- Recreational activities
  - Volleyball, tennis, ping pong, and basketball to build teamwork skills, physical health, and self-esteem;
  - Swimming, for girls;
  - Art sessions, including pottery, beadwork, origami, and papier-mâché;
  - Gardening and cooking;
  - Field trips to such places as state parks, skating rinks, and the zoo; and
  - Traditional dance groups perform during the annual Tet and Harvest Moon celebrations.

  Seventy boys and 15 girls participate regularly in the recreational activities.

Community Partners

Catholic Charities Archdiocese of New Orleans (Immigration and Refugee Services)

The Vietnamese Church Parish

The New Orleans Police Department

New Orleans Public Schools

Versailles Arms Apartment Complex

Families in Need of Services (Orleans Parish Juvenile Court)

- Life planning
  - Informal after-school discussions help youth reflect on issues in their lives. This component is more structured and focused during summer camp.
  - The youth coordinator and parish priests lead retreats for youth and their parents.

  Twenty-six boys and 15 girls participate regularly in the life-planning activities.
- Tutoring
  - The use of a highly structured and engaging remedial educational software program, PLATO, is the core of the after-school tutoring program.
  - When students are ready for the academic component of the program, their reading, language arts, and math skills are assessed with the PLATO Fastrack Test.
  - PLATO then provides students with a beginning grade level score in each skill area and an "individualized learning path" consisting of hundreds of PLATO lessons.
  - Field trips are rewards for measured progress in the PLATO programs.

  Twenty-six boys and 15 girls participate regularly in the computer tutoring sessions.

In addition to the after-school program, the VAYP offers a summer camp, where activities focus on life-planning sessions, rap sessions, and outdoor recreational activities.

Results

- Teens have become committed to improving themselves and their community and are helping each other do it.
- At the end of the school year, of the 26 boys in the tutoring program, three were back in school and three had begun the GED program. One boy has made great progress in a trade school.

- Of the 15 girls in the program, three girls who had been skipping school and failing are now making As and Bs, and four who were doing mediocre work, now make straight As. Two girls are now on the honor roll consistently and have graduated from the youth program.
- Seven boys who were on the verge of dropping out stayed in school, and four girls now attend a distinguished magnet school.
- Youth counselors and probation officers collaborated successfully to get one of the youth back into school and on track for the first time in years.
- The youth volunteer their time and energy to clean up, renovate, and plant flowers around the program site.
- For many of the youth, the annual summer camps were their only experience fishing and camping. The nightly life-planning sessions at camp resulted in their re-evaluating the life goals they had set the year before.

Getting Kids Involved

- Recreational activities are a time-tested method of attracting at-risk youth to a youth program. The team sports offered by the Vietnamese Youth Program initially attract many boys who would otherwise not have participated in any aspect of the program.
- The computer programs, especially PLATO, have caught the interest of these at-risk teens in ways that traditional classroom learning has not. The offer of field trips as incentives for progress in the computer work provides added motivation to many youth.
- The parents of refugee girls are often reluctant to allow them to participate in anything other than school, partly because they fear for their daughters' safety, and partly because they want them at home attending to household duties. Program staff met with parents to negotiate a balance between the daughters' needs and aspirations and the families' needs. In addition, staff assured the parents that the activities are always attended by at least one adult. For the girls' safety, staff and parents share the task of transporting them back and forth to the program.

Challenges Faced and Resolved

- Some participating youth have gotten into legal trouble.
    - ♦ The program maintains contact with these youth while they are incarcerated and welcomes them back to the group. One of the boys made a marked improvement in his outlook and actions and has stayed out of trouble since.
- Moving girls into the program was a challenge. The girls bond throughout the program and are sometimes not open to accepting newcomers, so outsiders tend to drop in and out of the program because they do not feel welcome.
    - ♦ Often the older girls (and boys as well) are given particular duties and responsibilities, such as tutoring the newcomers in the program. This breaks up the cliques.
    - ♦ Staff have started to draw in new girls slowly rather than in larger groups, which is less threatening to the girls already participating.
    - ♦ Those girls who have excelled at a sport or skill encourage and challenge the others, which enhances their self-esteem and defines their role as seniors, so they do not feel the need to compete with the new arrivals for territory in the program.
- Getting youth to participate in the program was sometimes difficult.
    - ♦ The program's three-tiered system, with sports and other recreational activities, helps draw in youth who might be intimidated by life-planning sessions, computers, or daily tutoring.
- Youth who are not in school or are not making the honor roll have not come as far as their peers in the program.
    - ♦ These youth are encouraged to contribute to community projects, such as working in the church and assisting with the New Year Festival each February. Despite a slow start, they get interested in improving themselves and soon develop motivation and a sense of responsibility.

- Girls weren't always drawn by the sports activities.
  - ♦ Swimming was introduced and has become a permanent part of the youth program. It is the girls' favorite sport and provides them with opportunities to build confidence and self-esteem. They also participate in volleyball and tennis.
- A major goal was to keep participating youth off drugs and hopeful that the investment they make in their education, themselves, and their futures will pay off.
  - ♦ The youth discuss their futures with staff, who help them develop realistic plans for achieving their goals, including skills training for jobs that may be meaningful and profitable.

Resources and Support

- Funding for three full-time staff positions, the PLATO computer tutoring program software, costs for recreational activities, arts and crafts supplies, office space, and transportation costs are provided by a four-year grant from ORR.
- Volunteers from the church and surrounding community provide a range of assistance, including chaperoning daily recreation and long trips and providing an open line of communication with the Vietnamese community.
- Contact and dialog with church leaders provides essential guidance for the program.
- The University of New Orleans allows the Versailles Asian Youth Program to utilize its swimming pool for $3 per person.

Community partner contributions:

- Catholic Charities Archdiocese of New Orleans, Immigration and Refugee Services, lead partner, administers and oversees the project and provides staff and office space.

- The Vietnamese church parish, Mary Queen of Vietnam, has donated the use of its large, enclosed parking lot for recreational activities. For example, the three-day lunar New Year celebration is held on church grounds.
- The New Orleans Police Department and New Orleans Public Schools work closely with program staff in many aspects of the youth work.
- Versailles Arms Apartment Complex contributes to the program by referring its Asian residents to the program for services.
- Families in Need of Services (FINS), a juvenile court program for youth with minor criminal infractions, has developed a partnership with the program. Youth and their parents sign contracts agreeing to participate in the Versailles Asian Youth Program for at least six months as an alternative to juvenile court. If a contract is broken, the youth must have a formal hearing before a judge.

Who To Contact

Dr. Susan Weishar
Vietnamese Youth Program
Catholic Charities Archdiocese of New Orleans
Refugee and Immigration Services
1000 Howard Avenue, Suite 1200
New Orleans, LA 70113-1916
Phone: 504-523-3755, ext. 2606
Fax 504-523-6962

Multicultural Eyes and Ears for a Safer Community

STRATEGY 7

Town Watch is contagious; when neighborhoods commit, crime has no choice but to submit!

A police captain
Philadelphia Police Department

Purpose

Crime and violence were on the rise and causing concern in Philadelphia in 1994. The city council response included mandatory revitalization of a Philadelphia tradition, Town Watch, in which citizens create a bridge between police and the community and help control crime by patrolling neighborhood streets and reporting suspicious activity.

At the same time, the city's refugees were discovering a need for community crime prevention because rising crime and victimization were making it increasingly difficult for them to thrive in their new communities. As authorities worked on revitalizing Town Watch throughout the city, they realized that language and cultural barriers were preventing the program's success within refugee communities.

City Managing Director's Office staff discussed the crime problems with representatives from the various MAAs and found that the refugees were interested in participating in a Town Watch. These staff then identified funds from the Targeted Assistance Program (TAP) that were already allocated to improve refugee safety and security and used those funds to pay for part-time staff for the MAAs to educate and recruit refugee residents. The result was a Town Watch program tailored to the cultural and language needs of refugee populations.

Program Structure

Staffing

- Philadelphia Town Watch Coordinator, City Manager's Office, administers the program.
- Philadelphia Police Department oversees training and distributes equipment.
- Every two years qualified candidates recruited by the MAAs undergo advanced training to become Town Watch volunteers.
- Three trainers from the city office and 23 community relations officers from the police department train the volunteers.

Activities

Town Watch training teaches the volunteers how to

- Classify and prioritize incidents in police terms,
- Be effective eyes and ears for the police by observing suspects and events, and
- Not confront criminals or directly involve themselves in crimes in progress, but to document and report critical information to police in a timely manner.

After training, the volunteers

- Observe and report to the police such activities as vandalism, car theft, disturbing the peace, and loitering;
- Address quality-of-life issues. For instance, when trash is a problem, the Town Watch members notify the sanitation department;
- Reach out to the refugee community. They educate them on using the 911 emergency system appropriately and taking steps to avoid being identified as easy victims — such as locking their doors and depositing money in a bank instead of keeping it at home;
- Act as liaisons for other community members and the police. This helps refugees overcome their reluctance to interact with police and increases their access to the police;
- Serve as interpreters for the refugees;
- Appear in court if necessary;
- Submit monthly reports to a police community service officer to provide statistics about Town Watch activities and accomplishments; and
- Meet once a month with their district's patrol community relations officer to submit records and results and to compare notes.

Results

Refugees are less fearful of the police, and police are more aware of the refugee groups living in their districts. Some examples noted by police:

Community Partners

City of Philadelphia, Managing Director's Office

Philadelphia Police Department

Refugee MAAs

- The Cambodian Town Watch effort in South Philadelphia was a valuable resource in solving a double homicide of two young refugees. Without an identified Town Watch leadership contact, the police would have had difficulties solving this crime.
- An Ethiopian community Town Watch participant gave such a detailed report of a homicide that the police captain asked where the volunteer learned crime reporting skills. This was the captain's first contact with the Ethiopian Town Watch group.
- The Refugee Town Watch has often provided police important information in solving gang-related crimes, a major concern among the Philadelphia Asian population.
- Refugees from the former Soviet Union became a vocal part of police/community parterships. Previously, they had attended community meetings but had never voiced their concerns.

Challenges Faced and Resolved

- Fear of seeking police assistance was the greatest barrier to refugee involvement in Town Watch.
  - ♦ The success of the program begins with volunteer recruitment by the MAAs and continues as Refugee Town Watch volunteers patrol their neighborhoods. Gradually the refugees' feelings of mistrust are replaced by feelings of belonging and participation in their new community.
- It was difficult to get recruits from the ethnic communities.
  - ♦ Communication was improved. The MAAs are key to the success of the Refugee Town Watch program. When they conduct community education programs on neighborhood safety and Refugee Town Watch activities, they are in a good position to seek out potential recruits.

Refugee Town Watch Prevents Crime

A barking dog is usually near the bottom of police priorities, but Town Watchers are trained to handle all complaints effectively by providing police with precise information. Their training teaches them to ask accurate questions in order to determine the exact problem.

In the case of the barking dog, a refugee Town Watcher investigating the complaint asked the key question: "Does the dog bark all the time?" The neighbor who had complained replied that the dog hardly ever barked. Upon investigation, it was found that the dog was barking because a man was abducting a woman. The call quickly became a much higher police priority, the Watcher provided the police with accurate and timely information, and an arrest was made.

Resources and Support

- The city general funds support a citywide Town Watch coordinator who is charged with developing and training all Town Watch groups. For the Refugee Town Watch, city funds also support three trainers and purchase supplies and equipment.
- The police department budget supports all the activities of the 23 community relations officers.
- TAP supplies federal grant funds to employ part-time staff who are hired by the participating MAAs.

Who To Contact

Donna Wolf
Managing Director's Office
1401 JFK Boulevard, Room 1430 MSB
Philadelphia, PA 19102-1683
Phone: 215-686-3483
Fax: 215-686-3479

Summer Refuge for Refugee Youth

STRATEGY 8

I don't know what you did with these kids over the summer, but the change is astounding; they're doing well in school and are motivated to learn English. We hardly recognize them!

A school counselor

Purpose

For Cuban refugee youth in Dade County, FL, the school year was a time when the schools provided them with work and service agencies provided them with the emotional and therapeutic support they needed. In the summer, they had the same needs, but no services were in place to fill them, and their parents were working full time.

In 1996, parents, the Department of Human Services, and the Office of Youth and Family Development Services worked together to develop a solution to the children's unprotected, unproductive days of summer.

These days, at-risk youth attend The Refugee Youth Summer Camp where they receive intense, supportive therapy to improve or maintain gains made through therapy during the school year. The summer camp setting provides a chance for staff to focus on each child's issues.

A secondary goal is to provide safe, affordable, summer recreational activities for the children of refugee families.

Program objectives include

- Promoting positive interactions between youth,
- Increasing social skills of youth participants,
- Broadening participants' awareness of Miami's cultural and artistic resources,
- Providing gang and drug prevention activities, and
- Providing a comfortable setting for program staff to interact with parents.

Program Structure

Staffing

- Three full-time social worker aides, with cultural and immigration experiences similar to the youth participants, lead activities.
- One full-time and six part-time youth counselors help youth sort out emotional issues while running recreational activities.
- One part-time clinical social worker helps youth work through social and emotional issues.
- A project coordinator supervises the summer program part time.

Activities

Youth create plays, compete on athletic teams, and tour museums, theaters, and parks.

- Students in the summer camp meet for 10 weeks, five hours a day. Each day is divided into three sections.
  1. Art and drama provide a wide range of options; during this time the youth
     - Go on field trips to the Miami Art Museum, Main Public Library, Art in Public Places—Metro Tour, Miami Beach Art Deco District, and a production of The Wizard of Oz;
     - Stage their own productions; and
     - Create their own art. For example, with the help of an artist, a tile company, and Home Depot employees, they learned tile-working skills and built a 30-foot by 16-foot tile mural along one wall of a racquetball court that had been the target of graffiti. Now if the graffiti returns, it can simply be washed off.
  2. Athletics and free-time activities, which include organized sports and trips to local parks.
  3. Counseling and psycho-educational groups, which support the youths' learning while meeting their psychological needs.
- Sixty-seven students from six Dade County middle schools participated in the youth summer program.

Results

- In a follow-up study of a random sampling of 30 youth, using report cards and interviews with parents, teachers, and school counselors, all 30 had maintained or increased their grade averages.
- The same study showed that all the students had improved their social skills.
- Although some of the 67 participants had been on the verge of dropping out before camp, all are still in school.
- A majority of the students made visible gains toward meeting treatment goals.
- Students had increased feelings of self-worth and belonging; these gains are shown through positive behavior changes reported by school staff and parents.

Community Partners

Office of Youth and Family Development Refugee Service Program of Miami Dade County

Dade County Public Schools

Miami-Dade Art in Public Places

Parks and Recreation

Department of Human Services

Challenges Faced and Resolved

- It was difficult to obtain sufficient transportation for program participants.
  - ♦ Program staff were able to acquire a passenger vehicle with grant money from the Florida Department of Children and Family Services.
- A federally subsidized lunch program for participants was often insufficient and was available for only eight of the 10 weeks.
  - ♦ Program staff purchased some lunches and obtained some donated lunches from community resources. Similar arrangements have been made for local provision of lunches in the future to avoid the problem.

Resources and Support

- The Florida Department of Children and Family Services funding covers staff and transportation costs; other expenses are covered by donations. At $740 per child, this program is cost effective, compared to similar therapeutic programs at $2,000 per child.
- Office of Youth and Family Development Refugee Service Program of Miami-Dade County, lead partner, administers the program, coordinates program activities, provides staff, refers clients, and conducts resource development.
- Dade County Public Schools provides curriculum support, referral, and materials.
- Miami-Dade Art in Public Places provides space, material, and trained volunteers.
- Parks and Recreation provides space, equipment, and materials.
- Department of Human Services provides a summer lunch program.
- Area restaurants, such as McDonald's, Taco Bell, Boston Market, and Kentucky Fried Chicken, donate food to supplement federally subsidized lunches.
- Area businesses, such as Tropical 98.3 FM, Amerilumber, Pepsi Cola, El Zol Radio, Home Depot, and Iberia Tiles, contribute supplies and training sessions. For example, Home Depot taught the children how to replace tiles for one of the service projects.

A Success Story

"Pedro," who was referred to the program because of dysfunctional classroom behavior and not passing one class the entire school year, is an example of a young person helped through the summer camp.

When Pedro first assisted younger participants he made fun of them and pointed out their weaknesses. Staff consistently worked with Pedro to help him develop empathy.

Pedro responded by offering apologies to his victims and assuming the role of a teacher. Pedro noted that the support he received from his youth counselor was the most valuable part of the summer experience for him.

School counselors report that his behavior has improved remarkably. He is now doing well in school and is motivated to learn English.

- Individuals make generous contributions of supplies and time.
- Paper products, soft drinks, paint, poster board, balls for various games, and materials for the mural project and art exhibit were donated.

Who To Contact

Ulysses Arteaga, L.C.S.W.
Refugee Youth Summer Camp
Refugee Family Services Program
Miami-Dade Department of Human Services
Office of Youth and Family Development
1401 SW 1st Street, Suite 101
Miami, FL 33125
Phone: 305-649-4063
Fax: 305-643-8555

YWCA to the Rescue

STRATEGY 9

We need to take the Welcome Wagon approach and educate the mainstream community as to how to prepare for New Americans.

Chief Charles Gruber
Elgin Police Department

Purpose

In 1992, in Elgin, IL, a group of Lao youth banded together as the Lao Posse in the schools in response to pressure and harassment from other cultural groups. The gang troubles in the Lao community spread quickly into several Illinois counties and even across the Illinois-Wisconsin border.

The Elgin YWCA was well-positioned to stop the growth of gang activity and to assist the families of gang members with their legal problems. Since 1979 the YWCA Refugee Project had been providing immigration, community, school, legal, job, and crime prevention services to more than 4,500 youth and adult refugees.

In 1993, the Elgin YWCA worked with the Elgin Police Department to develop their YWCA Refugee Crime Prevention Program. The goals of the program are

- To develop cooperation and understanding between the refugee community, police departments, and other agencies;
- To promote crime and gang prevention; and
- To provide public safety education.

Program Structure

Staffing

YWCA staff run the program.

- Director of community services handles administrative duties and oversees activities.
- Crime prevention and community and family liaisons conduct community outreach, coordinate substance abuse and gang prevention activities, help in planning and coordinating youth activities, and act as liaison to the court and the police department.
- Refugee youth program coordinator handles membership and volunteer development and coordinates daily youth activities and special youth and cultural events.

Activities

- A drop-in youth center for young people ages 10 to 21 provides a gymnasium, weight training, swimming, video games, billiards, and field trips.
- A supervised "youth room" gives youth a place to socialize and talk about concerns.
- Court and school mediation and advocacy are provided for families, as well as youth.
- Family counseling and intervention assists with intergenerational communication problems.
- Workshops provide information regarding legal, school, community, and governmental processes in the United States.
- Gang prevention activities, such as the "Youth vs. Law" volleyball games in which youth compete against law enforcement officers, help divert the youth from gangs.
- Gang prevention counseling is provided for troubled youth.
- Education, career, and employment counseling and job placement are provided to give youth direction and focus.
- Special events, such as the celebration of the Lao New Year in mid-April, are organized in cooperation with the Elgin Police Department.
- The youth perform traditional dances for special events.
- Twenty youth from a wide variety of backgrounds participated in a Youth Forum where they talked to the public about crime and violence.

Results

- Refugee youth gang activity has dwindled to a few minor isolated incidents.
- Understanding between the refugee community and the police has increased. The Lao youth have become comfortable interacting with police officers.

Community Partners

Elgin YWCA

Elgin Parks and Recreation Department

Renz Addiction Counseling Center

Elgin Gang/Drug Task Force

Elgin Police Department

- The Elgin Police Department recognizes the crime prevention program's contribution to the refugee community's increased understanding of the law and their rights.
- Refugee community members report feeling more secure.

Challenges Faced and Resolved

- There were financial obstacles to maintaining the project
  - ♦ Obtained funding from the United Way and the City of Elgin.
- Attracting gang members, as well as others, to alternative activities was sometimes difficult.
  - ♦ The YWCA sports and recreational activities, equipment, and facilities drew youth into the program. Once they arrived, the children learned of the many other activities and programs. The youth room, where they can "hang out" and talk about problems with the program coordinator, is especially popular.
  - ♦ "Youth vs. Law" volleyball games are very popular with both refugees and law enforcement officers.
- Maintaining support of the Lao community was a challenge.
  - ♦ Involving parents and elders of the community is key to success. In Elgin, one highly respected Lao community member promotes adult involvement in program activities.
- It was necessary to maintain the support of the broader community.
  - ♦ Publicizing special events, such as holiday celebrations and cultural events, fosters a positive cross-cultural relationship and keeps the community informed about program activities and successes.

Asset Forfeiture—and How You Might Use It

When law enforcement officers arrest an offender who has assets—either cash or property—that were illegally obtained, the authorities can convert the property to cash through auction.

State Asset Forfeiture Funds can sometimes be used for community programs. Some communities turn the funds over to the law enforcement agency that made the arrest, others earmark the money for libraries, schools, or other local uses. Law enforcement officers can use the funds for community crime prevention purposes, such as substance abuse prevention and intervention. To find out more, call your police department, your sheriff's department, or your city attorney's office.

Federal Asset Forfeiture Funds are not readily accessible for community programs because they are bound by a statute specifying use only for joint law enforcement operations with federal partners.

The book *Finding Federal Funds (and Other Resources) To Prevent Crime* explains creative, widely accessible ways to increase your funds for crime and substance abuse prevention and gives examples of communities that have used these methods. See Section 3, "Resources," for information about ordering this book.

Resources and Support

- The city and the United Way of Elgin provide $28,000 for the crime prevention/family and community liaison position, program and office supplies, administrative assistance, and space.
- Funds from the Drug Asset Forfeiture Money were used to establish the nearby recreation center, which is staffed by volunteers.
- Police volunteers participate in sports activities, chaperon at special events, and provide assistance to refugee families facing legal difficulties.
- Elgin Parks and Recreation Department provides the program with a variety of recreational activities.
- Renz Addiction Counseling Center provides recreational activities.
- One hundred thirty-five youth volunteers work a total of 300 hours every year.

STRATEGY 9

Who To Contact

Ann de Cruz
Community Service Director
YWCA of Elgin
220 East Chicago Street
Elgin, IL 60120
Phone: 847-742-7930
Fax: 847-742-8217

Sports and recreation have a healthy appeal for refugee girls and boys.

Preventing Crime by Overcoming Cultural Barriers

STRATEGY 10

This program is an invaluable resource to us. Atlanta is an ever-changing place, and the Bridging the Gap program has assisted us in dealing with these changes and in doing so has also caused a change in the attitudes of all parties involved.

Officer Marc Harrold
Atlanta Police Department

Purpose

"You just don't understand" used to be a common feeling between refugees and police in Atlanta, GA. Language barriers, perceived insults, and misunderstood non-verbal signals were getting in the way of justice. On the other side of the communication chasm, service providers were sometimes using meetings to lash out at police, to stereotype them and, at times, to browbeat them.

To improve communication and understanding among ethnically diverse communities, public and private organizations, and law enforcement, The Bridging the Gap Project, Inc., (BTG) formed the Diversity Training for Public Safety Personnel Program. The program, started in 1994, consists of diversity training sessions for law enforcement personnel and bimonthly meetings of the Multi-cultural Task Force.

Program Structure

Staffing

- A Georgia P.O.S.T. (Peace Officer Standards and Training Council) accredited professional lecturer conducts all training sessions.
- Ethnic specific panelists and presenters participate in training sessions.

Activities

Diversity training sessions are offered to public safety personnel at various law enforcement agencies and training academies throughout Georgia. Peace officers can earn two hours of academic credit for most of these sessions. Since 1994, more than 3,000 public safety personnel have attended and received credit for BTG training.

The sessions can be two hours to sixteen hours long, depending on the needs of the academy. The number of participants ranges from 35 to 150.

BTG has also developed numerous resources for diversity training. Currently, they have developed ten modules, three videos, and several cultural descriptions of various ethnic groups.

Meetings of the Multi-cultural Task Force are convened by BTG and law enforcement agencies to discuss cultural issues. Participation in most meetings earns two hours of academic credit.

Results

- Public safety officers participating in the training have consistently given the highest possible evaluation ratings.
- Officers and departments are requesting advanced training.
- Officers are now requesting meetings with community members.
- Officers are contacting BTG for assistance with cases and for technical assistance on cultural issues.
- Refugees are responding positively to contacts with police.
- Calls from refugees and immigrants to 911 have increased.
- More refugees are attending community meetings, and more meetings are being requested.

What Public Safety Officers Say About the BTG Diversity Trainings:

"Time well spent."

"It makes me want to get involved more and learn more. I feel eager to get involved and enthusiastic about learning about other cultures. Thank you for an outstanding course."

"Love to see this taught to cops!"

"Thank you. Very informative of what type of situation we will be facing."

"Bringing people from Russia, Somalia, and Vietnam was a bright idea—we gained first-hand knowledge about their culture—helping us create a good atmosphere between the police and their community. Good job!"

"This program should be mandated."

"This class is highly informative. It is very important that one learns how to recognize and deal with individuals and groups from other countries and cultures."

"I would like to have even more time to speak with more people of different cultures and races to learn about their cultures and how to properly interact with them."

Challenges Faced and Resolved

- It was difficult to develop a training module that would teach the importance of diversity while also respecting law enforcement culture.
    - ♦ In order to overcome this, BTG clearly defined police sub-culture and its influence on interaction with ethnic groups. This was accomplished through observation and solicitation of the law enforcement perspective.
- There was difficulty convincing law enforcement agencies from jurisdictions without a large immigrant or refugee community to enroll in diversity training.
    - ♦ BTG conducted successful training for agencies requesting help and then relied on referral to introduce the training to other departments.
- Particular departments and styles of enforcement had differing training requirements and needs.
    - ♦ Content and material are designed to meet the specific needs of departments.
- Recruiting credible representatives from immigrant and refugee communities to participate on panels and in small group discussions for trainings posed a challenge.
    - ♦ BTG researched the demographics of jurisdictions in order to ensure that immigrant or refugee communities were accurately represented at training sessions. They then recruited community representatives and trained them about the informational needs of law enforcement officers to prepare them for participation.

STRATEGY 10

Community Partners

The Bridging the Gap Project, Inc.

U.S. Attorney's Office-Northern District

U.S. Department of Justice (DOJ), Immigration and Naturalization Service (INS)

Georgia Human Relations Commission

Catholic Social Services, Inc.

Resources and Support

- Funding for staff, materials, and office facilities is provided by grants from the U.S. Department of Justice, Community Oriented Policing Services program (COPS) and ORR.
- BTG, lead partner, provides staff, office facilities, and materials development expertise.
- Police training academies provide facilities and equipment, as well as hotel and travel expenses, when necessary.
- The U.S. Attorney's Office-Northern District collaborates to fund and convene two-day training conferences.
- Immigration and Naturalization Service (INS) helps train law enforcement officers about immigrant processing and documentation and about the relationship between INS and local law enforcement agencies.
- Georgia Human Relations Commission collaborates with BTG on training, particularly diversity training, conflict resolution, and domestic violence in ethnic communities.
- Immigration and Refugee Services of America provides technical assistance on immigration policy changes and immigration training.
- Catholic Social Services, Inc. teaches "survival Vietnamese" to law enforcement officers and participates in diversity training.

Who To Contact

Gail Hoffman
The Bridging the Gap Project
c/o The Sullivan Center, Inc.
1615 Peachtree Street, NE, Suite 120
Atlanta, GA 30309
Phone: 404-872-9400
Fax: 404-872-4888

A Bridge to Success for At-Risk Families

STRATEGY 11

Leave the walk, the talk, the attitude, and disrespect at the gate. None of it means a thing to the horse.

Youth Equestrian Program Motto

Purpose

Some troubled Southeast Asian refugee youth in Modesto, CA, didn't seem to care about or respect themselves, each other, or anything else.

Staff at the Bridge, a Southeast Asian Refugee Services and Community Center Project of California State University (CSU)-Stanislaus and Modesto Junior College, decided that caring for animals might help these youth start caring for each other—and themselves.

In early 1997, with the help of volunteers and trainers, the Bridge staff started an Equestrian Youth Project. Modesto is not a rural community, so a youth project focusing on horses might have seemed unlikely, but staff and volunteers quickly found the resources to make their idea a reality.

The goal of the program is to modify aggressive behavior; to prevent crime and gangs; improve physical fitness, muscle tone, and coordination; and help youth learn respect and compassion for living creatures, interpersonal and teamwork skills, responsibility, independence, and self-confidence.

Although fairly new, this program has shown impressive results in a short period of time. The juvenile probation and juvenile courts acknowledge its value and are making referrals. Teachers throughout Modesto have begun involving as many refugee youth as possible in the project, and its university sponsor is looking into expanding it.

Program Structure

Staffing

- One full-time instructor/trainer teaches the youth how to care for and ride the horses.
- Five full-time volunteers assist youth in working with the horses.
- Community volunteers serve as guest speakers, conduct fundraising activities, and provide transportation, materials, and other general program support as needed.

Activities

- Eight to 15 youth spend two hours per week in the winter and five in summer at the Ceres Sports Arena, a professional rodeo arena. There they ride and care for horses, study the basics of agricultural science and livestock management, and learn about agricultural employment opportunities.
- Well-qualified instructors/trainers and volunteers help youth develop grooming, tacking, and riding skills.
- Mounted police work with youth at the arena, and both mounted police and patrol officers stop in to interact with youth at the arena and at the Bridge program. In addition, youth visit the police equestrian unit during work days to get to know the officers and to learn about their work.
- Youth take field trips to local farms and ranches to explore agricultural career possibilities.
- Guest speakers are invited to provide information on agricultural topics relevant to the needs of the youth.
- Participants keep a journal of their activities.

Results

- The youth now respect and admire the police and even write letters to them.
- In discussions with other service providers, program staff have confirmed that youth participating in the program have stopped engaging in minor criminal activities, such as graffiti and vandalism.
- Youth have learned to respect and care for living creatures. For instance, some youths' initial reactions to the horses were to pester and injure them. Now these same young people are concerned about the horses' well-being and are gentle and competent in caring for them. In fact, on one occasion when the students noticed one of the horses was pregnant, they hesitated to ride her, fearing they would injure her. This showed a marked shift in behavior.

Community Partners

CSU-Stanislaus

Modesto Junior College

Modesto Police Department

Stanislaus County Juvenile Probation Department

4–H

UC Davis Cooperative Extension

United Way of Stanislaus

- Communication between youth and parents has improved. Many parents are from rural areas in Southeast Asia and have experience in farming techniques. Now there is common ground for discussion. Parents are invited to attend and assist in program activities.
- Getting to know and understand the refugee youth provides cross-cultural knowledge for the American-born volunteers and helps them develop a positive attitude toward refugees.
- Being taken out to the arena, away from their neighborhoods into drug-free, neutral areas that are not "claimed" by any gang member, has helped the youth to develop a positive attitude toward the future.
- Overcoming the fear many youth have of horseback riding requires that they develop trust.
- Since the youth must remain focused and attentive while receiving instructions, they develop better listening and concentration skills and improve in school.
- Agencies that have not traditionally partnered or worked with refugee youth are collaborating on this project. For example, the partnership between 4–H and the Modesto Police has enabled both to see the benefits of collaborative projects.

Challenges Faced and Resolved

- An equestrian program can be expensive, requiring money for instruction, lesson horses, equipment, arena rental, insurance, and transportation.
  - ♦ These problems were addressed by
    - Cooperation among agencies/pooling resources,
    - Promotion of the program to the community and asking for its involvement,
    - Recruitment of volunteers and private donations, and
    - Successful application for grant funding.
- A limited number of horses are boarded at the arena.
  - ♦ The children take turns studying and riding.

STRATEGY 11

Sources of Horses

Finding horses for a refugee youth program is not as difficult as it would first appear.

The first step is to get a trainer who is sensitive to cultural differences and able to work with children. Look for trainers in the yellow pages or ask local stable staff for recommendations.

The next step is finding a place to board and ride the horses. Local stables and horse owners, and often local 4–H chapters, have the facilities and resources to sustain an equestrian program; your part is to reach out to them to develop a partnership.

- Epona's Place, a private stable in Florida, runs a therapeutic riding program for the benefit of the stable, as well as the children. Since horses must be exercised and groomed, having children ride and care for the horses saves the stable money by reducing the need for permanent staff. At the same time, the children benefit from contact with the horses and responsibility for their care.
- 4-H is always willing to help children become involved in agricultural and environmental issues and can be an outstanding and dependable source of funding and contacts for horses.
- A local foundation keeps the horses corralled for the Nez Perce Mounted Scholars program and permits the Native American children in the program to ride and care for them.
- Equine Rescue organizations rescue horses from the slaughter house and will donate older horses to therapeutic equestrian programs free of charge. The Thoroughbred Retirement Association in New Jersey works directly with Juvenile Services Department in Baltimore, MD, by donating horses and supplies for juvenile programs. To locate Equine Rescue organizations in your area, call the Humane Society Headquarters in Washington, DC, at 202-723-5730 or search the World Wide Web.
- Once you have your program, rodeo organizations can help sustain it. Often the rodeo will provide stable facilities and donate or discount arena time for riding; their benefit comes from the resulting positive public relations.

Resources and Support

- 4–H provided numerous volunteer hours, public donations, and a one-time start-up grant of $1,500, which was enough to cover initial fees, such as transportation and riding helmets.
- CSU-Stanislaus provides staff, accounting services, grant proposal assistance, and student volunteers through Community Service Learning, an internship program.
- Modesto Junior College provides student volunteers through Community Service Learning, along with agricultural staff assistance and facilities on campus.
- Modesto Police Department refers youth to the program and provides sponsorship through the equestrian unit.
- Stanislaus County Juvenile Probation Department provides volunteers and refers youth.
- The University of California (UC)-Davis Cooperative Extension provides classroom and instructional material, guest speakers, field trip assistance, and liability and accident insurance.
- United Way of Stanislaus provides financial support.
- Community members volunteer and provide donations.

Who To Contact

Carla Emig
The Bridge, Site Coordinator
620 Paradise Road, F-102
Modesto, CA 95351
Phone: 209-571-8430
Fax: 209-667-3324

Portland Puts Gangs in Check

STRATEGY 12

The chess tournament is more exciting than being in the gang!

An eighth grade program participant

Purpose

It's tough enough for youth to thrive in school when they know the language and the culture and they're raised in a safe environment. Imagine the obstacles for students who are surrounded by gangs, have parents who don't speak English, and lack understanding of U.S. culture.

For many Portland, OR, refugee youth who were in this situation, gangs, drugs, and crime seemed much more enticing and attainable than graduating from high school. To keep these youth in school and to help them achieve while they are there, the Portland Police Bureau and social workers began a tutoring program for refugee youth in 1994 called "Get That A."

Staff found that youth who came to the Asian Family Center for assistance with their school work often stayed to play chess with their friends. These informal afternoon games evolved into the "Make That Right Move" program where learning chess strategy teaches the students to think ahead, to anticipate crucial moves, and to set long-range goals. Getting ready for and competing in the tournament teaches youth commitment, the value of patience and practice, and the challenge of improving themselves.

Program Structure

Staffing

- Volunteer police officers tutor, mentor, and referee chess games.
- The Asian Family Center staff provides tutoring.
- Asian high school and college students volunteer as tutors.

Activities

- At the tutoring sessions, students do their homework with the help of a tutor who speaks their native language.
- After their homework is finished, students play chess or checkers with their friends.
- Youth compete in a chess tournament, with prizes for participants.

How Does a Game of Chess Help?

Do not underestimate the value of a game of chess. In an entertaining way, it provides a student with confidence, as well as strategies for future planning and goal setting. When this occurs, kids have no need for gangs, drugs, and violence.

Officer Preston Wong
Portland Police Bureau

Results

- During the first year, as many as 12 students at a time came in for help. Now, about 30 students, from second grade through high school, regularly attend the program.
- Seventy-five percent of the youth participants are gang and crime free. They perform better in school and understand more about Western culture, the English language, and the role of police officers.
- Through chess, students learn to think, plan ahead, and set long- and short-term goals.
- Many refugee parents have learned to trust the police as they become better acquainted with the officers.
- Crime reporting has increased as the level of trust has increased.
- Refugee adults are seeking out police officers to discuss concerns.

Challenges Faced and Resolved

Challenge	Resolution
■ Funding is difficult to obtain.	♦ A small grant from Multnomah County provided for basic program needs.
■ Few students were attending the program.	♦ The chess tournament attracted students. Prizes were awarded for first, second, and third place.
■ Students were reluctant to ask questions.	♦ Tutors who spoke the students' native language were present. Students became more comfortable when they saw other students struggling with the same issues.

Resources and Support

- Funding for basic school supplies, chess and checker sets, refreshments, and tournament prizes is provided by:
  - A grant from Multnomah County, and
  - Private donations.

12 STRATEGY

Community Partners

Portland Police Bureau

Asian Family Center

Portland Public Schools

Rose City Village housing project

Portland refugee youth find chess tournaments absorbing, as well as exciting and challenging.

- Volunteers from the Police Bureau and the Asian Family Center coordinate program activities.
- Safeway and the Sunshine Division of the Portland Police Bureau contribute food and drinks.
- Staff members and volunteers from Portland Public Schools consult with teachers to determine student weaknesses and academic requirements so students can focus on these areas during study sessions.
- The management of the Rose City Village housing project provides space for the tutoring group.

Who To Contact

Preston Wong
Gang Enforcement Team
Portland Police Bureau
449 NE Emerson Street
Portland, OR 97211
Phone: 503-823-2098
Fax: 503-823-4162

Working With Refugee Community Elders

- To establish initial contact with refugee community elders, ask your local resettlement agencies if they would be willing to set up meetings for you.
- Representatives from the resettlement agencies will probably want to participate in these meetings, and you can benefit from their knowledge of the culture.
- Be sure to arrange for translators—the resettlement agencies may be able to provide them.
- If there are several ethnic groups in your community, you should meet with elders from each group separately. At the initial meeting you can get information to enable you to maintain ongoing communication.
- Be friendly and respectful and listen carefully to what the elders are saying. Your attention to what they say will encourage them to pay attention to your points.
- Try not to become impatient if refugee elders digress from the point of discussion, remember that digression can often provide valuable, if unexpected, information. Bring them back to the main point in a way that respects their opinions.
- Talk to the elders first. They are the leaders of their households. By talking with them first, you show respect for their position in the family.
- Never promise refugees something that is out of your power. Broken promises destroy any trust that has been established.
- Try not to debate with or contradict an elder. Bring your diplomatic skills to the meeting. By honoring the opinions of the elders, you will earn their respect and that of the community.
- Respect the values of the culture even if they're not your own or do not seem appropriate in the larger community.

Seniors on the Watch

STRATEGY 13

Now we feel more in charge of our safety and well-being and have more direct contact with public safety.

A Vertical Eye Watch floor representative

Purpose

When two elderly residents were accosted in the park behind their apartments in Oak Park, MI, the victims' family members decided it was time for more building security.

- Family members of the victims complained to board members of the apartment complex and requested increased security;
- The building administration met with the town mayor, who referred them to the public safety department;
- As a result of the planning meetings, in 1995, building management and residents adapted the traditional neighborhood watch crime prevention strategy and community policing techniques to form the Vertical Eye Watch (VEW), a neighborhood watch program for high-rise buildings.

The project goals are to raise awareness about crime prevention and safety and to prevent crime at the building complex through organizing community residents.

VEW was originally intended to assist the 300 elderly, predominantly Jewish residents in two apartment buildings. To accommodate an influx of Russian refugees in 1993, the program was soon expanded to include the third building in the complex and the Community Center. The three residential buildings now house 470 residents, half of whom are refugees from the former Soviet Union.

Program Structure

Staffing

VEW has no paid staff. The volunteer-run program is a true partnership of public safety officers,* apartment complex staff, and community residents.

- The building administrator, social work staff, and a Russian translator manage the program.
- One public safety officer, the emergency services coordinator, is available at all times to the residents of the building, and patrol officers assigned to the area stop in occasionally to visit with residents.

- Volunteer floor representatives, identified by badges, organize resident watch schedules, contact the building office or public safety officers if problems arise, and report any concerns at monthly meetings.
- Residents volunteer as Resident Eye Patrol members.

  * In Oak Park, MI, police officers are called public safety officers because they are cross trained in firefighting, police work, and Emergency Medical Services.

Activities

- Each resident has a tag that is placed on the door at 10 p.m. and removed by 11 a.m. each day. A missing tag at night or a visible tag during the day might indicate a problem. Floor representatives will knock on the door or call the apartment resident to determine if anything is wrong.
- Public safety officers train residents on safety issues in bimonthly meetings. Translators ensure that everyone can participate and understand the material.
- Resident Eye Patrols ensure safety by remaining alert to any changes or unusual occurrences.
- Complex administrators, public safety officers, and a Russian-speaking translator developed manuals in English and Russian to orient the residents to the program's safety procedures.
- The administrative staff, floor representatives, residents, and the translator attend monthly meetings.

Results

- The newest group of Russian-speaking refugees is now taking an active part in VEW activities. Sixty-five percent of all the floor representatives are New Americans.
- Attitudes of residents have changed dramatically. Administrators and public safety officers report that the majority of residents are more aware of safety needs, actively communicate their needs and concerns, take personal responsibility for the safety of their community, and feel more secure within their apartments and community.

C.A.S.E.—Create a Safe Environment

Staff and resident concerns regarding violence on the apartment complex premises led to the development of C.A.S.E. When issues arise that relate to violence, workshops are conducted by the building administrator, social work staff, the clergy, and a police liaison. Topics include the potential eviction of a tenant, a disgruntled employee, or a violent act or death on the premises. This program has helped residents and staff feel safer.

- The use of the door tags to monitor the floors has helped save lives and has made the residents feel more secure and less isolated. Sometimes the resident has simply forgotten to remove the tag, but more often someone is sick or has fallen and is unable to get to a telephone to call for help.
- The emergency services coordinator reports that the number of calls for police service to these residences has decreased as a result of the VEW presence.
- Police report that calls regarding suspicious activity in the surrounding area including the park behind the buildings have decreased significantly because of VEW presence.
- Police are calling on the VEW translator for assistance in community issues.
- Residents have expanded their community policing role and now, after an eight-hour training session by police, enforce handicapped parking regulations on the residential grounds.
- The refugee residents have become so involved in their community they developed and maintain a model recycling program.
- VEW won the Silver Circle Savvy Award at the City, County Community Marketing Association Conference in Washington, DC. It was also showcased by the National League of Cities at the Good Neighbor Great Cities Showcase of City Programs.

Challenges Faced and Resolved

- The influx of Russian-speaking refugees into the buildings caused confusion in the watch program.
    - ♦ A Russian-speaking interpreter and translator lessened confusion and enabled non English-speaking residents to express their concerns in the regular town meetings and bi-monthly VEW meetings.
    - ♦ The VEW manual was translated into Russian, making it easier for the refugee floor representatives to understand and follow the information presented at the monthly meetings.

Community Partners

Prentis and Teitel Federation Apartments

Oak Park Public Safety Department

Municipal Cable TV-15

- Few new residents were participating in the program.

♦ Watch members stopped pressuring new residents to participate in the program. More new residents joined after they saw the positive results of the Watch. Ninety-eight percent of the elderly population now participate in the door tag process, and everyone cooperates with building security issues.

Resources and Support

- The budget for this project is very low; there are no operating expenses because the volunteer residents do most of the work and administration is carried out from the complex offices. The only expenses are incidentals, such as the door tags.
- Apartment building staff manage the program.
- Oak Park Public Safety Department provides training, program development, and community policing services, such as patrolling.

Responsibilities of Floor Representatives

- Get to know all residents on the floor.
- Represent the common needs and concerns of the residents on the floor to promote their health and welfare.
- Present ideas from the floor at the resident council meetings.
- Visit and welcome new residents to the floor within five days of their arrival.
- Invite new residents to attend the resident council meetings.
- Provide follow-up information to new residents regarding apartment complex dining room procedures.
- Encourage respect for building cleanliness.
- Report excessive noise or quiet on the floor.
- Follow-up on the door tag program by checking tags at appropriate times and reporting concerns to the office.
- Report to the office anything out of the ordinary, such as mail build-up under apartment doors, an open door, not seeing a resident for days, or strange odors and sounds.
- Meet periodically with public safety officers and other floor representatives to discuss concerns and brainstorm solutions.

- Municipal Cable TV-15 developed a video explaining the creation, development, and impact of the Vertical Eye Watch program for community education and publicity.
- To express their appreciation and feeling of partnership, apartment complex residents not only volunteer their services in the complex, but they have also developed an annual tradition called "Christmas in July" when they gather baked goods, fruit, and sweets and deliver them in baskets to the Department of Public Safety.

Who To Contact

Iris Mickel
Administrator
Prentis Federation Apartments
Jewish Federation Apartments, Inc.
15100 West 10 Mile Road
Oak Park, MI 48237
Phone: 248-967-4240
Fax: 248-967-1557

Delivering Hope, Not Drugs

STRATEGY 14

We're not in the neighborhood gangs. We're in Alice's [project manager] gang. We help people.

A 14-year-old Vietnamese program participant

Purpose

In 1988, when staff at the Newcomers' Network witnessed refugee children being used to deliver drugs near the Refugee Community Center in Clarkston, GA, they knew it was time for community action. They quickly recruited volunteers and created a mini summer program for six- to 17-year-old young people to keep them involved in positive and healthy academic, social, and physical pursuits.

Today, ten years later, the network's youth projects involve more than 400 youth each year in activities that provide constructive and engaging alternatives to drugs. Projects include an After-School Program, a One-To-One Tutoring Project, Summer Camp, training by local law enforcement officers, and the Service-Learning Leadership Club (SLLC).

About 60 youth per year, of all ages, make positive differences in their community through the SLLC. The strategy is to get youth involved building better communities. Children respond readily to the opportunities offered by this program; some children as young as nine are taking leadership roles.

By planning and carrying out community development projects, the young people gain self-confidence and learn practical skills, such as idea development, organizing, fund raising, budgeting, and publicity management, as well as gain a sense of civic responsibility.

Program Structure

Staffing

- A full-time program manager oversees all Newcomers' Network youth program activities, including the SLLC.
- The SLLC children and youth work with the program manager to plan and carry out the service projects.
- Community volunteers and part-time staff sometimes help with meetings and special events.

Membership Details

- All refugee and immigrant children in the community between the ages of seven and sixteen are encouraged to join the SLLC. Children are informed through fliers, announcements at other Newcomers' Network activities, and a telephone tree. Several children have taken the responsibility to recruit other children into the club.

- The club meets at the Newcomers' Network community centers, which are within easy walking distance of the children's homes.

Activities

- Activities are chosen one of in two ways:
  1. The coordinator surveys the community to determine a wide range of possible service activities and resources available. These options are presented to the children at the club meetings.
  2. The children are guided through an interactive brainstorming activity in which they identify their concerns about the community.
- The children decide on projects and resources needed, then develop action plans and carry them to completion with guidance from staff members and volunteers.
- The children have completed four service projects:
  - Twenty children conducted a pedestrian safety campaign including a puppet show, songs, games, and posters;
  - Ten children completed a peer tutoring program;
  - Fifteen children created a butterfly garden; and
  - Fifteen children conducted a recycling program.

Results

- The Pedestrian Safety Campaign won Grand Prize in the National Safe Kids Challenge, a national competition sponsored by National Safe Kids.
- Through the Campaign, the children successfully encouraged an apartment complex to construct more speed bumps to increase safety.
- One of the children from the Campaign was selected to fly to Washington, DC, where she met and interviewed her representative to Congress and advocated for pedestrian safety. For this event, she not only learned interviewing skills, but she also learned how to communicate clearly for media interviews.

How To Develop a Service Learning Project

Success will not just happen. Thoughtful planning is a must.

- Before the first meeting, research what types of projects are possible, practical, and needed by the community.
- Pick a meeting location that will attract the type of youth you are targeting.
- Depending on the age, size, and location of your group, different brainstorming/community needs assessment techniques are most useful. Here are some popular ones:
  - Create a treasure hunt for children. As they run through the community going from clue to clue, they must answer written questions about safety, environmental issues, and health. Afterwards, while they are enjoying their bounty, they and the program manager discuss the problems they identified in the community and decide which ones are most important to them.
  - Distribute a checklist of healthy behaviors and decide which ones are true and which ones are not true of the community. Checklist statements might include, "we have a smoke detector in our apartment and check the batteries every month," or "I feel safe when I am at school." The children can discuss the ones that are not true in their communities. They can then decide which ones they care about most and choose one to be a goal to work toward.
  - Propose several project ideas to the children; they choose one.
- Once youth have picked their goal, they will need constant encouragement and must be steered toward the materials and resource people who can help them. This step needs to happen as soon as possible after they choose their goal, while interest and enthusiasm are high.
- You will need to develop a curriculum to accompany each goal or category of goals, such as the environment. Outside resources to help you develop the curricula might be the library, the Internet, and groups that help children or have community service messages, such as the Red Cross, law enforcement, the American Friends' Service Committee, and the Board of Health.
- Have children follow a given curriculum over several sessions using interactive activities that are relevant to their situation. Make sure each lesson is fun for the children and not just educational, or the youth will drop out of your program. These sessions can include issues such as mini-proposal writing, public speaking, working with the media, and budgeting. All of these lessons should be elementary, interactive, quick paced, fun, and presented in a way directly relevant to the task at hand.
- Recognize the youth and publicly praise them for their good work. In addition to raising their self-confidence, awards ceremonies are good advertisements for building community support.

Community Partners

Newcomers' Network

Safe Kids of DeKalb County

Clarkston and Chamblee Police Departments

Plan It Green

- The Campaign was featured on the front page of *The Weekly Reader*, a periodical for elementary school children.
- As a result of their participation in SLLC, the children continue to express interest in civic events and community service.
- Fifteen older children taught many younger ones English, arts and crafts, safety skills, environmental topics, and sports.
- Children have learned how to effectively tutor their peers.
- Children have learned to write mini-proposals.
- Children have developed a greater sense of civic responsibility.

Challenges Faced and Resolved

- In order to learn responsibility and gain leadership skills from this program, the children need to plan and carry out appropriate projects of their own choosing.

♦ The project manager and volunteers work with club members to

- Provide consistent encouragement to ensure that the evolving plans take into consideration community needs, available resources, and what can reasonably be achieved, and that projects committed to are completed;
- Teach children successful methods for developing ideas;
- Guide children through the processes of organizing, fund raising, budgeting, and publicity management; and
- Mentor youth and help keep them on task.

- Some children want to dominate or bully others within and outside of the club.

♦ The children come up with a list of guidelines for behavior that everyone agrees to follow. Infractions of these rules are not tolerated.

- Finding space has been difficult given personal safety issues for the children, fire codes, and transportation restrictions.

- ♦ Activities are structured so that all are playing important roles and everyone is actively engaged.
- ♦ Schools and community centers are being used.
- ♦ Staff are looking for a larger space within safe walking distance from the children's homes.

Resources and Support

- In 1997, the SLLC received start-up funding from the Georgia Department of Human Services (DHR). DHR provides primary funding for the after-school programs and the summer camp program.
- City of Atlanta Arts Clearinghouse donates art supplies.
- Georgia Cooperative Extension Service donated free seeds and saplings for the community garden.
- Atlanta Food Bank provides snacks for the children during the year.
- Local schools provide space for some activities, refer students to the program, and provide updates on children's progress. Indian Creek Elementary gave the project classroom space for one year for an after-school program in which service learning was a part. Cary Reynolds Elementary arranged for the SLLC to perform its puppet show and safety skits for all of its children in pre-kindergarten through third grade.

Community partner contributions:

- Newcomers' Network, lead partner, provides one full-time staff person to run the Refugee Youth Project, which includes SLLC. Older youth volunteers and interns play an invaluable leadership role.
- Safe Kids of DeKalb County provides materials for teaching about unintentional injuries and volunteers to back up the children's presentations.
- Clarkston and Chamblee Police Departments provide officers and materials for training the youth on safety issues.

- Plan It Green provided environmental expertise for the butterfly garden and the recycling campaign, as well as supplied numerous volunteers and a high-quality environmental education curriculum.

Newcomers' Network Treasure Hunt

1. Find all the people with birthdays in the same month as yours. This is your team.
2. As a team, follow the clues to find questions. When you find a question, think about the answer and write it down. When you get to the end you'll find the treasure!

CLUE	QUESTIONS
1. Up, up to the sky. Just a little higher and I could fly. But then I go down in a swing, only to try all over again. Can you find me? **(Swing)**	Do the kids use the playground here? What would make the playground fun? What would make the play ground more safe? Write your answer on your paper.
2. What are the things in the road that make the cars go slower? Find the one closest to Newcomer's Network. **(Speed bumps)**	Do the children and the cars obey the rules of the road? Are the children safe or do they sometimes get hit by cars? Write your answer on your paper.
3. Find it! We open these to let the air in. **(Window)**	Can little children accidentaly fall out of the upstairs windows in Woodgate? Write your answer on your paper.
4. Find it! I make noise when it's hot and smoky! **(Smoke detector)**	My family checks the smoke detector batteries every month. True or false?
5. Find it! What is black and white and read all over? **(Mailboxes)**	What do people do with the mail after they have read it? Is there a place to recycle junk mail? Write your answer on your paper.

Who To Contact:

Susan Somach
Newcomers' Network
3647 Market Street
Clarkston, GA 30021
Phone: 404-299-6273
Fax: 404-299-6218

6. Find it! Where people cook food. **(Kitchen)**	Women and girls are the only ones who should cook. True or false? It's OK for a husband to hit his wife if she doesn't please him. True or false? It's OK for boys and men to have more than one girlfriend at a time. True or false?
7. Find the biggest tree on this side of Newcomer's Network.	Are there places for animals to call home in Woodgate Apartments? What do animals need to survive? What do people need to survive? Write your answer on your paper.
8. Go to the place where children wait for the bus to go to school. **(Bus stop)**	Circle one: I feel safe when I am waiting for the school bus. True or false I feel safe when I am at school. True or false
9. Most of the earth's surface is covered with ________. Find it! **(Swimming pool)**	When you are by the pool, you have to follow the rules. Swimming is a whole lot of fun, but only when you follow rule number one. What is it? Do the children follow the rules when they are swimming? How could we make swimming safer? Write your answer on your paper.
10. Go back to the place where the children can go to get help with their homework to find your surprise. **(Newcomers' Network)**	

Teenagers, Police, and Ethnic Communities Gang Up on Crime

STRATEGY 15

I have met new people, many people from other countries and cultures. It's cool. I like it.

An Explorer Post youth participant

Purpose

Gangs are a growing problem in St. Louis, both inside and outside refugee communities. But teenagers, refugee community members, and police aren't just sitting around worrying about it. First, community members asked the International Institute of St. Louis to study their current crime prevention system. Institute researchers found that, although there were several crime prevention service providers, there was no coordinated effort to involve multiethnic groups.

To begin involving the different ethnic groups, the International Institute and the Police Department began International Police Explorer Post 9203, a crime prevention program for 27 to 40 teenagers. The 14- to 19-year-old Bosnian, Ethiopian/Eritrean, Lao, and Vietnamese youth learn about law enforcement careers, while serving as valuable community service volunteers.

Program Structure

Staffing

- Project director provides part-time supervision.
- Youth services coordinator works half-time with the Explorer Post.
- MAAs and volunteer refugee community leaders provide guidance and community liaison services.
- There are four regularly scheduled volunteers, three from the police department.

Activities

- Explorer youth participate in weekly meetings where a volunteer police officer teaches them about crime investigation, fingerprinting, building searches, traffic stops, and community laws. They are tested on their knowledge.
- Explorers participate in community service projects.
- Explorers participate in social activities, such as picnics and dances, with youth from other Explorer posts.

Results

- Youth are making friends across ethnic boundaries.
- Youth have taken the initiative to start raising funds on their own behalf.
- Refugee parents feel comfortable with their children being involved the program.
- The program has built positive relationships between police, the community, and youth through joint activities.
- The Explorer Post is a popular place to be. Despite strict guidelines for membership, there are more interested parents and young people than available memberships.
- Participation in community service projects is high. Attendance at events is near perfect—with 12 to 15 youth regularly involved in each event.
- The first community service project was accomplished within one month of the first meeting. Explorers provided crowd control at the Variety Club Telethon, a local community-wide charity fund-raising project.

Challenges Faced and Resolved

- Being unfamiliar with scouting programs, community leaders and parents were first puzzled and then somewhat suspicious about the program purpose and the young people's role within it. It was feared that the young people might be viewed as spies.

♦ Staff addressed this issue by
  - Developing an informational brochure,
  - Publishing native language press releases in newsletters/newspapers and church bulletins, and
  - Holding individual interviews with prospective parents and members (utilizing interpreters) prior to the first meeting.

Problem	Solution
■ The multiethnic, multilingual nature of the project presented numerous language problems during the recruitment process. (Members speak and read five languages and use three alphabets.)	♦ Most spoken communication is followed with written confirmation. Interpreters facilitate communication with parents. When setting document production schedules, extra time is allotted for translation.
■ Meetings were originally scheduled for a weeknight and parents were reluctant to let their children attend because they wanted weeknights reserved for school work.	♦ The meeting day was changed to Saturday.
■ Too few police officers were available to attend meetings for the new post.	♦ Social work practicum students from local universities volunteered initially. Now there are two additional police volunteers, including one female.

Resources and Support

- Funding for two part-time staff is provided through a three-year grant from ORR.
- International Institute of St. Louis, lead partner, coordinates and oversees the program through the services of two part-time staff members.
- St. Louis Police Department provides a van for transportation and volunteers to attend the meetings, plan and lead activities, and serve as role models for youth.
- Refugee community leaders and MAAs provide translations of materials, recruit youth for the Explorer program, liaison with the refugee communities, and provide project guidance.

Community Partners

International Institute of St. Louis

Boy Scouts of America

St. Louis Police Department

MAAs

- Boy Scouts of America provides insurance, as well as project and activity ideas.
- St. Francis de Sales and Sigel Community Education Center provide facilities.
- Various restaurants provide food for special events.
- Photocopy businesses donate the cost of copies.
- Volunteers from the local community keep records, serve as liaisons between the post and other organizations, and developed an evaluation tool.

Community Service Project Ideas for Refugee Explorer Youth

- Assist in crime prevention education programs.
- Undergo fire department training and install smoke alarms in high-crime, high-risk apartment buildings.
- Drill peepholes in residents' doors in high-crime, high-risk apartment buildings, as indicated by police, and show residents how to use them.
- Bring stuffed animals to nursing homes, chat with residents, perform native songs or dances, and engage in guided discussion of the experience.
- Collect donations of prepared food from restaurants for a homeless shelter and learn about homelessness from shelter staff.
- Clean up a neighborhood.
- Plant trees to help convert a vacant lot into a park area.
- Help with natural disaster relief efforts.
- Help promote safety campaigns, such as a campaign to end the use of guns on New Year's Eve.
- Team up with police for police/community athletic events, such as soccer games.
- Assist with crowd control, directing traffic, and security at major events and parades.

15
STRATEGY

Who To Contact

Jane Knirr
The International Institute of Metropolitan St. Louis
3800 Park Avenue
St. Louis, MO 63110-2514
Phone: 314-773-9090
Fax: 314-773-6047

International Explorer Post youth proudly display colors from their native cultures.

A Storefront With a Difference

STRATEGY 16

I want to be a police officer, just like you!

A Cambodian child speaking to Senior Corporal Paul Thai, the first Cambodian-born police officer in the United States

Purpose

If victims won't come to you, go to them. That is the philosophy of the Dallas Police Department. In the early 1980s refugees were settled in substandard, dilapidated apartment complexes with minimal social services and were often victimized by burglaries, assaults, robberies, and vandalism. Yet few refugees reported these crimes because of language and cultural barriers and mistrust of authorities.

In 1984, the City of Dallas opened a unique storefront of multicultural crime prevention and social service programs in the heart of the Southeast Asian community in East Dallas. The police department staffed the center with three public service officers from Vietnam, Laos, and Cambodia, and then began to meet its goals of

- Developing a partnership between the City of Dallas and refugee populations,
- Reducing victimization,
- Enhancing quality of life, and
- Enabling refugees to become more self-sufficient.

Program Structure

Staffing

- The storefront is currently staffed by eight officers and has a bicycle unit.
- Dallas refugee service providers were consolidated into a coalition housed within the storefront to provide services under one roof. These service providers were the East Dallas Counseling Center, the Dallas Cambodian Association, the Vietnamese MAA, the Dallas Buddhist Association, and the Dallas Public Schools.

Activities

- The social services provided in the storefront include
  - food and clothing distribution referrals,
  - job referral and placement for newly arrived refugees,
  - court and health care translation and interpreter services, and
  - public assistance information.

Community Partners

Dallas Police Department

Baylor Hospital

The U.S. DOJ Office of Weed and Seed programs

Boys & Girls Clubs

Refugee MAAs

- In addition, the storefront provides multi-language crime prevention programs, which encourage mutual cooperation between the refugees and the police. Activities and programs include
  - A five-language crime stoppers hotline;
  - American citizenship classes;
  - Youth mentoring and tutoring programs;
  - Three Boy and Girl Scout troops;
  - Two Explorer Posts;
  - Five-team soccer league made up of Vietnamese, Laotian, Cambodian, Amerasian, African-American, and Hispanic youth;
  - Creation of crime watches and neighborhood associations; and
  - Translation and distribution of multi-language crime prevention literature.

Results

- During the first two years of this project (1985-1986) the rate of reported crimes from the refugee community increased dramatically, as did the number of arrests and incidents of recovered property. The rise in reported crime is a positive result of the storefront, as it fostered the development of trust by refugees, encouraged officers' foot patrols, and improved offense-gathering techniques within the community.
- Three years after the storefront opened the rate of reported crime fell by 17 percent.
- Increasing numbers of Asian Americans have become Dallas police officers.
- The storefront partnership successfully involves a variety of education, social service, and criminal justice agencies.
- In 1986, the Public Broadcasting System's Peabody Award documentary, "Starting Over In America," profiled the Dallas storefront operation and its effectiveness in addressing the needs of refugee families.

- In 1987, the storefront was selected by the Police Foundation as one of the best inner-city crime reduction programs in the United States.
- During its 14 years of operation, the storefront has received more than 12 awards from local community organizations.

Where To Look for Storefront Facilities

Many mainstream organizations and businesses understand the wisdom of investing in a safe community and helping New Americans make a smooth transition into life in this country. Here are some creative ways of finding space for a police-refugee storefront.

The Westminster, CA, Police Department provides easy access to services in a shopping mall in "Little Saigon." Police contacted the owner of the main shopping mall, who donated space to gain a police presence in the mall because community fear of crime was affecting business.

Eventually, the landlord subsidized this resource center by charging slightly more rent to the other stores in the mall. These businesses gladly support the resource center because the increased police presence made it safe for people to shop there. They also found that people came to the center for the services offered and stayed to shop.

The city of Lowell, MA, requests proposals for storefronts. Landlords and business owners in low-income, high-crime areas who have extra space bid on the storefront. Many of them absorb the cost. These storefronts are used by police as their base of operations and are staffed 16 hours a day by community volunteers.

The St. Paul, MN, A Community Outreach Program (ACOP) storefront is located at the center of a large housing project where most of the city's refugees live. It obtained a city public housing grant to support its facility.

In Phoenix, a hospital and the public utility company, among others, donate space for police storefronts.

A very effective location, usually donated, is within offices where refugee services are provided. In Davenport, IA, police are based in the Refugee Resettlement Program. In Boston, the police liaison to the refugee community started out in the office of the Vietnamese American Civic Association, an MAA. And in Lincoln, NE, the storefront is in the Asian Community and Culture Center.

- Police, refugee community members, and refugee service providers in Dallas continue to commend this storefront and its ongoing efforts to keep Dallas crime free and ensure that refugees feel safe in their neighborhoods.
- As one of the pilot refugee/law enforcement storefronts in the United States, and as an outstanding example of local police initiative, this program has served as a model for the development of others around the country, in particular, in Westminster, CA.

Challenges Faced and Resolved

- The first major challenge was to overcome the mistrust and the language and cultural barriers between law enforcement officers and refugee communities.
  - ♦ The department hired and trained qualified Southeast Asian public service officers to staff the storefront and eliminate these barriers.
- In the early days of the program, officers in the Dallas Police Department had difficulty accepting and understanding the need for a police storefront for the Southeast Asian community. This traditional "police culture" was a barrier that initially kept the refugees and police from working together to make the storefront a success.
  - ♦ The involvement of the refugees in crime prevention and the social service components of the storefront created a higher level of trust between the law enforcement officers and refugees and helped eliminate the barriers.
  - ♦ This new relationship between the police and refugees resulted in police officers becoming more sensitive to the needs of the residents.
  - ♦ Traditional law enforcement officers found that policing was made easier as communication and trust developed.

Resources and Support

- The storefront and staff are currently sustained through the general funds of the City of Dallas.
- Friends of the East Dallas Storefront, a nonprofit organization that solicits and allocates funding for refugees needing assistance, is an important source of funding, as well as in-kind services.
- Citizens provide donations and charitable gifts for additional programs.
- Baylor Hospital nurses and hospital instructors routinely include police as they make daily visits in the community. They also provide ongoing cultural sensitivity training for police, as well as identify community problems, such as domestic violence. The police advise the nurses on legal issues.
- The U.S. Department of Justice Office of Weed and Seed programs, made up of a variety of social service and youth service agencies in East Dallas, provide technical training and information to assist officers and storefront service organizations in meeting the needs of the refugee community.
- Boys & Girls Clubs provide mentoring and sporting activities for refugee youth and facilities for officers involved in the Police Athletic League and other activities.
- Refugee MAAs provide technical assistance, such as transportation and counseling, and make referrals to the storefront.

Who To Contact

Sr. Cpl. Paul Thai
East Dallas Police Storefront
4545 Bryan Street
Dallas, TX 75204
Phone: 214-670-5517
Fax: 214-670-7888

SEAL Teaches Skills for Success

STRATEGY 17

I now realize the importance of our history as a people and that it is my responsibility to pass it on to the younger children.

A former gang member, now a program peer mentor

Purpose

As Hmong youth become "Americanized," they adopt American cultural values, practices, and ideals. Unfortunately, as they experience pressure to fit in with their American peers, many find the group support they need in gangs.

As a result, in 1988, the La Crosse Area Hmong MAA (HMAA) developed the Southeast Asian Leadership Youth Program (SEAL) to empower and educate refugee youth. By teaching skills in social adjustment, independent living, career exploration, conflict mediation, anger management, and prejudice reduction, SEAL staff and volunteers encourage youth to

- remain in high school and graduate,
- continue higher education or training, and
- become productive, well-adjusted, economically and emotionally self-sufficient members of the community.

Program Structure

Staffing

- Program director provides part-time oversight of the program.
- Four part-time peer assistants/mentors provide peer support and mentoring.
- Volunteer tutors from local colleges provide tutoring services.

Activities

- Students meet one-on-one with HMAA staff to form relationships with adults who are positive role models.
- Classes of 15 to 20 students are held two evenings a week for two hours.
  - One evening is devoted to classroom instruction and tutoring in independent living skills, such as budgeting, home management, employment readiness skills, community resource awareness, higher education and financial aid, juvenile law, gang prevention/intervention, and leadership development.
  - The second evening is focused on school work, including tutoring and homework assistance.

Community Partners

La Crosse Area HMAA

La Crosse School District

La Crosse County Human Services Department

La Crosse Police Department

- Students often come a third day, when staff assist them with community activities. For instance, they work with the Sierra Club on environmental projects or conduct fundraising for child abuse and neglect prevention education, neighborhood clean-up, etc. Sometimes this extra day is used for social events focusing on the development of the students' social skills.

- Several SEAL participants have served on the Multicultural Youth Council, whose mission is "to reduce racism and prejudice through non-violent educational efforts." Youth from diverse cultures present panel discussions about cultural differences and similarities and racism and prejudice to schools and civic groups.

Results

- More than 300 youth have participated in the SEAL program since its inception.
- Of the gang members who have been involved in SEAL, five percent have broken off all connections with the gang, which included changing their friends and associates, stopping criminal activity, and dressing differently. Ninety-five percent have stopped criminal activity.
- Ninety-eight percent of SEAL participants graduate from high school.
- Approximately 88 percent pursue higher education or training.
- SEAL won an award from the National Association of Counties in 1991 as a highly effective, culturally sensitive, and cost-effective program meeting the needs of at-risk youth.
- Southeast Asian community members now realize the need to provide parents with training on how to prevent and solve their children's behavioral problems.
- Many youth are court-ordered to attend SEAL because the program helps them resolve their problems and offers them a needed support system.
- The Multicultural Youth Council has increased awareness of social issues in the mainstream community.

STRATEGY 17

The Family Is Key

To provide effective services to at-risk refugee youth and families, the entire household must be involved. This type of education along with supportive programming empowers families to bring about positive and lasting change.

Denis Tucker
Coalition Coordinator

Challenges Faced and Resolved

■ Due in large part to the culture's traditional views on the role of children and youth in society and on the responsibilities of elders in educating and disciplining the children, there was a lack of interest and support for the program from the Southeast Asian communities.

♦ The attitudes of parents and community leaders have changed because of

- SEAL's efforts to educate the public about the program, and
- The obvious, positive changes in youth as a result of SEAL participation.

■ Relationships between Asians and police were extremely strained.

♦ Closer communication between the HMAA and the police on many issues regarding youth, such as cultural sensitivity and awareness of refugee concerns, has helped to diminish the tensions between the Asian community and the police department. In addition, the court sentences some offenders to the SEAL program.

■ Funding is always a challenge.

♦ Publicity efforts and a track record of success have resulted in increased funding sources.

Getting Parents Involved in Youth Programs

- Get to know the entire household through home visits, accompanying parents to PTA meetings and conferences, sponsoring culture-specific special events with parents as volunteers, and other activities.
- Make the youth program an important topic of discussion at board meetings and other gatherings where parents are present.
- Utilize clan or tribal representatives and leaders to encourage involvement of their members. Meeting with individual clans or tribes helps to educate them on the youth program, as well as to encourage their support.
- Promote involvement in the program through workshops specifically for refugee parents.
- Publicize the need for the youth program through local radio broadcasts.
- Make sure your program is family-based and culturally sensitive.

Once interested, parents make excellent partners in a youth program. They can tutor, especially in subjects such as math and science, and mentor youth. They can tell stories and teach crafts, art, music, dance, cooking, history, and language. This participation brings youth and their parents closer together and fosters a knowledge and appreciation of their own culture.

Resources and Support

- Primary support for SEAL is provided by local and national foundations, which provides funds for program staff, classroom facilities, and supplies for the social skills training events.
- The local job training agency in La Crosse provides grant funding.
- Community and local colleges provide volunteers to tutor and supervise tours and events.
- Local community volunteers, speakers, and others provide ongoing support and in-kind contributions.

17 STRATEGY

Who To Contact

Denis Tucker
Executive Association Director
La Crosse Area HMAA
2615 George Street
La Crosse, WI 54603
Phone: 608-781-5744
Fax: 608-781-5011

A Seal outing.

Healthy Families, Stronger Communities

STRATEGY 18

I never thought the things I know and do are important. Now I feel I have skills I can be proud of. I am very important in my family's life.

A program participant

Purpose

Refugee women in Seattle, WA, felt there had to be a better way to serve newly arrived women facing the task of adjusting to a new life and a new culture. Existing social service agencies were not prepared to address the unique needs and barriers of newcomer refugee women. Their most pressing needs were on-site child care, transportation assistance, ESL classes integrating women's topics and concerns, and domestic violence victim advocacy.

Realizing they could use their own perspective on the refugee resettlement experience to help other refugee women, these leaders founded the Refugee Women's Alliance (ReWA) in 1985. A nonprofit, community-based organization, ReWA provides networking, educational, and support services to refugee and immigrant women to help them achieve self-sufficiency.

The main goals of the program are

- To provide legal, housing, medical, and social services advocacy for bilingual/bicultural victims,
- To provide community outreach and education,
- To help prevent victimization and end domestic violence, and
- To facilitate networking.

Program Structure

Staffing

- Of 25 full-time professional staff speaking 20 languages, seven are dedicated exclusively to domestic violence victim advocacy.
- Each year, more than 100 community volunteers provide program support in the form of ESL tutoring, child care, office support including desktop publishing, legal assistance, clothing banks, and interpreting and translating services.

Activities

Primarily serving homebound women who are Cambodian, Lao, Mien, Hmong, Vietnamese, Chinese, Ethiopian, Somali, Eastern European, and former Soviets, ReWA

STRATEGY 18

Take a Closer Look at Domestic Violence and Refugees. . .

Isolation is part of the pattern of domestic abuse, and battered refugee women can be more isolated because of language and cultural barriers, loss of their social network and support system, and lack of information about services. Many will not go to a shelter for cultural reasons, but even if they do, sometimes they are turned away or leave the shelter early because staff aren't equipped linguistically to help them.

In some countries battering is not illegal, so victims may not know that it is legally wrong in this country and that assistance is available.

. . .and What You Can Do To Help

- Make your victim advocacy, shelter, and legal services accessible by providing translators (Never use family members as translators!), recruiting multilingual and multicultural staff and volunteers, and providing transportation as needed.
- Conduct training sessions and targeted outreach efforts to change community attitudes about domestic violence and to eliminate stereotypes that refugee women are uneducated, passive, or childlike, or that they come from a culture where domestic violence is acceptable. There is no typical battered refugee woman.
- Provide support to rebuild lives through referrals to culturally sensitive mental health counseling, job skills training, and permanent, safe shelter.
- Use your own judgement when taking cultural issues into consideration. Batterers will sometimes use "culture" as an excuse for violence and abuse.
- Remember that she has probably endured terrible experiences in her homeland and on her way to this country. Understand that in escaping the battering, she may be alienating herself from her religious and ethnic community, as well as her family, because of shame, stigma, and traditional values that often hide, deny, or minimize family violence. Know that she may be subjected to intense pressure from friends and relatives to endure the abuse and keep the family together at all costs.

- Provides cultural and linguistic support to individuals;
- Provides safety planning, shelter advocacy, legal and immigration referrals, and emergency assistance;
- Facilitates discussions on such topics as safety planning, the cycle of violence, self-esteem, and women's roles at weekly victim support group sessions for refugee and immigrant women— where on-site child-care, refreshments, and bus tickets are provided;
- Provides training and education on the causes and effects of domestic violence and the impact of domestic violence on the refugee and immigrant community; and
- Advocates an end to family violence by building coalitions with law enforcement, prosecution, schools, and other service providers.

Results

- The number of domestic abuse situations has decreased.
- More than 90 percent of ReWA's domestic violence clients can articulate an individualized safety plan for themselves and their children, including information about protection orders, confidential shelters, and other domestic violence resources.
- When a batterer treatment program was offered by ReWA, fewer than five percent of the participants re-offended during the course of treatment.
- ReWA was recognized by the City of Seattle in 1995 for innovative services.
- ReWA has served more than 900 refugee and immigrant victims of domestic violence since 1985.
- ReWA advocates provide more than 200 hours of community education every year to service providers and groups in the refugee and immigrant communities.

Challenges Faced and Resolved

- One challenge was developing and presenting an education and outreach program designed to prevent domestic violence in ethnic communities.
  - ♦ ReWA created "Maintaining Healthy Families," a community education model that addresses domestic violence in ethnic communities.
- Victim advocacy and batterer treatment services being offered within the same agency created some problems.
  - ♦ ReWA worked with a partner agency, the Asian Counseling and Referral Services, for two years to develop an effective transition plan for operating victim and batterer services at different sites, while expanding services for both groups.

Resources and Support

- Mainstream domestic violence advocacy and shelter programs provide shelter and referrals.
- Other refugee and immigrant service agencies provide referrals and employment services.
- Seattle Police Department provides referrals and cross training for ReWA.
- Public health clinics and hospitals provide referrals.
- More than 100 community volunteers provide a wide range of program support.
- Northwest Justice Project offers a weekly family law clinic on-site at ReWA.

Primary support for ReWA, including staff and facilities, is provided through grants from these organizations:

- ORR, through the Washington State Office of Refugee and Immigrant Assistance,

- City of Seattle, Department of Domestic Violence and Sexual Assault,
- King County, Women's Programs, and
- Local private foundations.

Who To Contact

Sue Wilkes or Beruke Giday
Refugee Women's Alliance
3004 South Alaska Street
Seattle, WA 98108
Phone: 206-721-0243
Fax: 206-721-0282

Creativity plays an important role in the refugee family ESL classes at ReWA.

Gangs to Clubs

STRATEGY 19

The project brings kids, parents, and the school together to find out what the problems are and what we can do to help our children stay in school and succeed.

Parent of a program participant

Purpose

In the early 1990s the news in Providence, RI, was filled with stories of crime and youth gangs. Refugee youth were dropping out of school in alarming numbers and some were becoming involved in the gangs. In a town meeting, refugee parents, school officials, community leaders, and law enforcement officials met and devised a plan for decreasing the threat of gang violence while improving the quality of life for refugee youth.

As a result, in 1992, the Mayor's Council on Drug and Alcohol Abuse (MCDAA) created the Southeast Asian Youth and Family Development (SAYFD) project to bring all crime, gang, and drug prevention efforts for Southeast Asian youth into one collaborative, city-wide effort under the umbrella of the Southeast Asian American Advisory Council. Today, activities for parents and youth include a Summer Academy, a Dropout Prevention/Tutoring project, Parent Training sessions, and a very successful gang prevention and intervention program, Gangs to Clubs.

Originally created for hard-core gang members, Gangs to Clubs now focuses on middle school youth. Staff found that the hard-core youth are less receptive to service programs and that working with younger at-risk students is more effective, since their connections with the gangs are not so firmly established.

This innovative program focuses on both the needs and strengths of at-risk refugee youth. By fostering self-esteem, a sense of direction, pride, and a sense of belonging, Gangs to Clubs provides youth with positive choices and attractive alternatives to fulfill the same needs.

Program Structure

Staffing

The Indo-Chinese Advocacy Project (IAP), an experienced ethnic service organization, runs the Gangs to Clubs program.

- Two full-time staff members from IAP administer and coordinate the program.
- A police liaison from the Advisory Council coordinates activities and transmits information between the police department and Gangs to Clubs staff.

- Many community members volunteer time to help make the club a success, such as teachers, who promote the club to the students, and police officers, who often sponsor and participate in activities.

Activities

- Once a week after school, 140 at-risk middle school youth meet in clubs.
- Club members are responsible for organizing and running their own activities, while staff simply monitor the meetings.
- The youth determine their club's identity, rules for participation, officers, and activities budget.
- Members participate in awareness, character, and skill-building exercises; take field trips, and enjoy outdoor activities.
- All 140 participants meet six times a year in formal life-coping skills training sessions. Guest speakers from various organizations make presentations about decision making, gang prevention, cultural understanding, conflict resolution, violence avoidance, substance abuse prevention, and pre-employment/job readiness.
- For hard-core gang members, the project organizes football games.

Results

A 1996 SAYFD evaluation survey showed many significant improvements in the lives of the participating youth and in the community as a whole:

- In 1993 over half the refugee population surveyed felt the gang problem was very serious; in 1996 that number had declined to 14 percent.
- In 1993 over half the refugee population surveyed felt there was an increase in weapons carried by Southeast Asian youth in schools; in 1996 the number had declined to 10 percent.
- Asian gang violence stopped. The police department's football games represented the first time in the history of Providence's Southeast Asian gangs that the two major gangs came together to play and talk without violence.

Virtually all the Southeast Asians surveyed now feel that it is safe to walk in their neighborhood during the day, and most feel safe at night. They also stated they believe that their neighborhood conditions would continue to improve.

STRATEGY 19

Community Partners

The Mayor's Council on Drug and Alcohol Abuse

The Indo-Chinese Advocacy Project

The Providence Police Department

The Providence Department of Recreation

Challenges Faced and Resolved

- It is difficult to transport children to and from club activities.
    - ♦ Volunteers often provide transportation. In addition, SAYFD obtains community donations to cover much of the transportation costs.
- The original grant from the Administration of Children and Families, U.S. Department of Health and Human Services, was discontinued due to federal budget cuts, but staff obtained substantially reduced funding through a grant from ORR.
    - ♦ While the loss of funding has limited SAYFD's other components, the Gangs to Clubs project sustains itself through monetary and in-kind donations from community members.

Resources and Support

- Gangs to Clubs is self-sustaining; financial support for SAYFD is being provided by ORR through 1999.
- IAP, one of the SAYFD service providers, administers the Gangs to Clubs program.
- The Providence Police Department provides parent training and crime prevention training.
- The Providence Department of Recreation provides sports facilities and transportation for field trips.
- All Providence middle schools donate meeting space.

STRATEGY 19

Finding Peace on the Football Field

The highlight of the police department's involvement in the Gangs to Clubs program was a recent series of football games played by gang members. As dozens of the city's most violent opposing gang members played together on the same field, self-confidence was boosted, and gang violence was reduced because gang members worked out their emotions on the football field. Though girls are not on the teams, they support the games and are also showing less violent behavior.

The first-place team displays its tournament trophy in the Providence City Hall.

- Surrounding area colleges, community volunteers, and the Socio-Economic Development Center provide support for SAYFD as a whole, which is coordinated by the MCDAA.
- Program staff solicit funding at the local and national levels, as well as encourage donations and in-kind support from community members.
- Congressional representatives and local government officials have been very useful in developing the program, community support, and funding.

Who To Contact

Howard Phengsomphone, Project Director
Mayor's Council on Drug and Alcohol Abuse
591 Charles Street
Providence, RI 02904
Phone: 401-421-7740, ext. 334, 336
Fax: 401-421-9243

Coping Through Outreach

STRATEGY 20

COPE has been and will continue to be a great help to our officers simply because the communities began talking to us and began to trust us as police officers more than they did in the past.

A Smyrna
Georgia police officer

Purpose

How do you cope with unique refugee community crime prevention needs? Atlanta area law enforcement agencies believed that existing service agencies didn't understand the difficult tasks faced by peace officers. At the same time both service providers and law enforcement felt that each could be more sensitive to the difficulties of the other. To solve these problems, law enforcement requested that the Bridging the Gap Project, Inc. (BTG) form the Community Oriented Policing and Education Program (COPE) in 1996.

With COPE, law enforcement serves as the primary partner in a collaborative effort to provide crime prevention information to refugee communities. The program provides a range of education and outreach services to the ethnic communities, local law enforcement agencies, social service providers, corporations, and schools.

Program Structure

Staffing

- Fifteen full-time staff members are fluent in twelve languages — ten are community outreach specialists, one law enforcement consultant, three administrative staff, and one recruiter for volunteers.
- More than 180 volunteers provide interpreting and translating services in 78 languages. Additional volunteers support the program by conducting research and data collection, assisting with office tasks, and establishing and maintaining neighborhood watch programs.

Activities

The COPE program is divided into three central initiatives:

- Bilingual recruitment of interpreters and translators, volunteers, and bilingual applicants for careers in law enforcement.
- Outreach activities for Haitian, Korean, Laotian, Latino, Somali, Chinese, and Vietnamese communities, which consist of

- Convening Community Enrichment Training sessions, which are regular meetings for refugees and immigrants, and often law enforcement officers, to share information and solve problems together. Outreach workers also use these sessions to assist refugees in understanding the laws and legal system.
- Monitoring five language-specific telephone hotlines for reporting criminal activity.
- Creating and distributing community orientation materials in more than six languages.
- Presenting ESL courses to assist in opening the lines of communication with law enforcement.
- Furnishing employment and family referrals, as needed.

In its first year and a half of operation, COPE presented 66 Community Enrichment Training sessions for more than 2,000 ethnic community members and law enforcement staff and 44 Community Enrichment Training sessions for more than 1,000 refugee community members without law enforcement participation.

- Services for law enforcement agencies
  - Provide law enforcement agencies access to COPE-operated Community Outreach Centers in the local area. At these centers, officers can meet with local refugees and immigrants and discuss crime and crime prevention. COPE also allows law enforcement officers to operate certain approved programs out of COPE Outreach Centers, such as the Gang Intervention and the Violence Education Program.
  - Provide interpretation and translation services.
  - Interpret and translate for law enforcement officers during follow up on crime incidents.
  - Forward information from the community to supplement police information regarding crimes.
  - Develop community oriented policing strategies.

- Provide P.O.S.T. certified training sessions for law enforcement officers on topics including diversity, using interpreters, and race and ethnicity. COPE trained more than 1,000 officers at 39 separate trainings in the Atlanta metro area in the first 18 months of program operation.
- Assisted Atlanta area Asian police officers in establishing the Asian Police Officers' Association.

Results

- Law enforcement officers and refugees are communicating better and beginning to develop trust. For instance, in one gang-ridden area that previously lacked a law enforcement presence and where the COPE outreach specialist was threatened on a daily basis, residents now regularly participate in community meetings with law enforcement officers. In addition, the outreach specialist is getting requests for information and assistance instead of death threats.

Connecting Successfully With Your Police Department

A community-based agency shares many of the same goals as local law enforcement agencies.

- Involve all affected parties in planning, as well as implementing, community policing and crime prevention services.
- You and your organization are a valuable resource for law enforcement agencies. Explain specifically to police how your assistance will make their job easier.
- Respect the police department's hierarchy and chain of command or you might be viewed as threatening.
- Know that the police are there to help you. If you do not truly believe that police as a whole are concerned and want to help people, it will be evident in your demeanor and make the connection you want nearly impossible.
- Remember that the police, like everyone else, are very busy. For many, developing community partnerships is accomplished in addition to their regular work and often during their private time.

Community Partners

The Bridging the Gap Project, Inc.

Numerous Atlanta area law enforcement agencies

U.S. Attorney's Office-Northern District

Asian Police Officers' Association

- Three of the areas where COPE maintains Outreach Centers have developed neighborhood watches and resident associations.
- Increasing numbers of local law enforcement agencies are contacting COPE staff for technical assistance.
- COPE has recruited 94 bilingual citizens for positions in law enforcement agencies. Sixty recruits are in various stages of the process and three have been hired by local police agencies.
- The number of Community Enrichment Training sessions requested by law enforcement agencies and the ethnic community grew from 12 in the first six months to 32 in the second six months, and demand continues to increase.

Challenges Faced and Resolved

- Refugees' lack of trust of uniformed authorities is an obstacle to community oriented policing in many refugee communities.
  - ♦ Community Enrichment Training sessions have assisted law enforcement officers and refugees to communicate and begin to develop trust.
- Since COPE serves a five county metropolitan area where many different languages are spoken it requires a substantial investment in staff.
  - ♦ For smaller communities, or those where fewer languages are spoken, the program is easily separated into components so it can be implemented according to the financial resources of any agency.

20 STRATEGY

COPE requires extensive resources because it serves a five county metropolitan area where many different languages are spoken. You can develop a program with similar goals, using fewer resources.

In working with refugees and immigrants,

- You might start with one minority group and add others as resources allow; or
- You can start with part-time staff; or
- If there are fewer languages spoken in your community, you will need a smaller staff.

In working with law enforcement agencies,

- You might start working with one department, and
- Use your successes to develop resources so you can work with additional departments in time.
- Again, if you have only one police department to work with, you will need fewer resources.

Use this outstanding program as a model to help you develop a similar one according to your resources, or call COPE to request training or technical assistance.

Resources and Support

- Funding for all staff and two of the Outreach Centers is provided by the U.S. Department of Justice, Community Oriented Policing Services.
- Local apartment owners and management donate space for three of the five Outreach Centers.
- Numerous Atlanta area law enforcement agencies provide a wide variety of resources, including materials, expertise, and meeting space, and make use of COPE services in working with New American communities.
- U.S. Attorney's Office-Northern District of Georgia coordinates training sessions for the law enforcement community.
- Department of Immigration and Naturalization Services educates the community regarding immigration law through workshops coordinated by COPE staff.
- Asian Police Officers' Association and COPE provide mutual outreach and technical assistance.
- Volunteer services help sustain the program.

20 STRATEGY

Who To Contact

Jarrette Burckhalter
The Bridging The Gap Project, Inc.
c/o The Sullivan Center, Inc.
1615 Peachtree Street, NE, Suite 120
Atlanta, GA 30309
Phone: 404-872-0555 or 404-872-1444
Fax: 404-872-4888

Laotian Outreach Specialist at Community Outreach Center.

SECTION III

RESOURCES

Materials

Materials and Resources Developed and Used by the Twenty Partnership Programs

The International Institute of St. Louis produced a video, "International Police Explorer Project," that is a summary of its Police Explorer Post project. To get a copy of the video, or for more information, contact Jane Knirr at 314-773-9090, or send $10 to cover costs (payable to International Institute) to Jane Knirr, International Institute of St. Louis, 3800 Park Avenue, St. Louis, MO 63110.

The Refugee/Law Enforcement Collaborative Resource Center in Dallas will send free copies of its video and materials to help you set up a similar resource center. Write or call Ron Cowart, Dallas Police Department, 4925 Worth Street, Dallas, TX 75214, 214-670-4881.

A videotape describing the WINGS project is available for $10. And a Domestic Violence handbook in Vietnamese, Spanish, and English, designed for use in the state of Iowa, is available for $5. For questions or to order, contact Nora Dvorak, Refugee Resettlement Office, 1706 North Brady, Suite 208, Davenport, IA 52803, 319-324-7913.

The Bridging The Gap Project, Inc., has developed many resources to help provide diversity training for law enforcement.

MODULES

- *Policing in a Diverse Society* (2 hours)
- *Using Interpreters to Your Advantage* (2 hours)
- *Building Collaboratives in Immigrant and Refugee Communities* (2-4 hours)
- *Survival Vietnamese for Law Enforcement* (7 weeks, 2 days/week, 3 hours/day)
- *Police Sub-culture* (1 hour)
- *The Difference Between Race and Culture* (4 hours)
- *Immigration and Documentation Verification* (2 hours)
- *Responding to Hate Crimes in Ethnic Communities* (2 hours)
- *Drug Abuse Resistance Education Activities With Immigrant and Refugee Youth* (2 hours)
- *Gender and Sexual Orientation Issues* (2 hours)

VIDEOS

Cultural Diversity Training: 1996 Centennial Olympic Games

Policing in a Diverse Society

American Law Enforcement and You

MATERIALS

Ethnographies of various ethnic groups

Ethnology comparing five ethnic groups and police sub-culture

For pricing information or to order, contact Gail Hoffman, The Bridging the Gap Project, 1615 Peachtree Street, NE, Suite 120, Atlanta, GA 30309, 404-872-9400, (fax) 404-872-4888.

The Versailles Asian Youth Program

For the Life Skills component of its youth program, the Versailles Asian Youth Program (VAYP) in New Orleans uses a curriculum from Advocates for Youth in Washington, DC. You can buy this curriculum or get a catalog of its materials by calling 202-347-5700.

The PLATO remedial educational software program, produced by TRO Learning, Inc., is used extensively by VAYP. To receive a catalog or to talk with a company representative, call 800-869-2000.

The Service Learning Leadership Club will provide you copies of its curricula at cost. Contact Alice Hunter, Newcomers' Network, 3647 Market Street, Clarkston, GA 30021, 404-299-6273.

Refugee Women's Alliance (ReWA) has developed materials that are available for purchase at cost through Lauback Literacy Action at 1320 Jamesville Avenue, Box 131, Syracuse, NY 13210, 315-422-9121.

- *Family Talk Time: A Curriculum for Refugee and Immigrant Parents* (1992, 120 pp.), $10.00.
- *From Classroom to Community: Building Leadership and Advocacy Skills in the ESL Class* (1995, 40 pp.), $4.00.
- *Celebrating International Women's Day—A Curriculum Sample* (1996, 8 pp.), $1.00.
- *Family Violence—A Curriculum Sample* (1996, 10 pp.), $1.00.
- *Family Tutoring: A Family-Based Curriculum for Refugee and Immigrant Parents* (1996, 226 pp.), $15.00.

Materials and Resources From the National Crime Prevention Council

Outreach to New Americans (ONA)

ONA was established in 1993 by NCPC in partnership with ORR and the Bureau of Justice Assistance, Office of Justice Programs, U.S.

Department of Justice to assist communities like yours to build refugee/law enforcement partnerships for crime prevention.

Project staff can provide you with or direct you to written materials, and sometimes videos, on crime prevention, coalition building, working with youth, resource development, cultural diversity, and almost any other topic that might be of assistance to you.

The partners also sponsor a national conference each year where law enforcement officers, refugee community leaders, and refugee service providers from around the country have an opportunity to share ideas about successful programs, creative resource development, solutions to problems, and to serve as a national network for future information sharing.

Project staff sometimes travel to communities around the country to assist in developing a dialog between law enforcement and refugees or to conduct workshops at state and national conferences to promote refugee/law enforcement partnerships. Staff have also trained a group of law enforcement officers and refugees, called the Peer Assistance Network, to do the same. This group is a resource in itself; see below for more information.

To discuss your community's needs and how ONA can best serve you get in touch with ONA project staff at NCPC, 1700 K Street, NW, Second Floor, Washington, DC 20006-3817, 202-466-6272, fax: 202-785-0698, e-mail: jama@ncpc.org or jwanmery@ncpc.org.

The Peer Assistance Network

The success of law enforcement/refugee partnerships around the country has been phenomenal. Refugee community leaders and law enforcement officers alike are delighted with the results of their positive work together. Many are eager to share their enthusiasm, knowledge, and skills with other communities to help refugees and law enforcement work together.

A select group of law enforcement officers and refugees have come together as the Peer Assistance Network (PAN) in order to do just that. With the skills they acquire in training conducted by NCPC staff, PAN members are able to facilitate community strategizing meetings, conduct trainings and workshops, and make effective presentations to promote refugee/law enforcement partnerships.

To inquire about PAN services, get in touch with Outreach to New Americans staff at NCPC.

Publications

The National Crime Prevention Council has many extremely useful publications, three of which will be especially helpful to you in developing and sustaining refugee/law enforcement partnerships.

- *Building and Crossing Bridges: Refugees and Law Enforcement Working Together* highlights effective strategies for law enforcement and refugee communities to build partnerships that enhance community safety. Describes ways in which the two groups can reach out to each other and how effective working relationships can be managed. Drawing on experiences at 17 sites across the nation, the book talks about a wide range of cultural, social, legal, and criminal justice issues. 60 pages, paperbound, $14.95, 1994.
- *Lengthening the Stride: Employing Peace Officers From Newly Arrived Ethnic Groups* lays out ways police departments can hire and retain members of ethnic minorities. Addresses opportunities, benefits, issues, challenges, and innovative solutions, especially with newcomer groups. 50 pages, paperbound, $14.95, 1995.
- *Finding Federal Funds (and Other Resources) To Prevent Crime* summarizes strategies that state-level groups have found effective in securing funds for prevention programs and elevating prevention on the policy agenda. Includes valuable evaluation checklists for policy and program level prevention efforts and a list of agency contacts for state-level inquiries on federal funding sources. 44 pages, paperbound, $12.95, 1997.

To order any of these reports, or for a catalog of NCPC publications, call 800-NCPC (6272)-911.

Programs

Two outstanding NCPC youth programs are

- Teens, Crime, and the Community (TCC), a community-based program whose purpose is to engage teens as crime prevention resources in their schools and communities. TCC combines education and action. The education component consists of a textbook to be used in more traditional school settings and a curriculum designed especially for community-based programs. Teen-led action projects conducted in the school or neighborhood involve youth in crime prevention or victim assistance activities addressing local needs. For more information, contact TCC staff at NCPC or visit the TCC Web site at www.nationaltcc.org.
- Youth as Resources (YAR) is a locally-based program that empowers young people to demonstrate their resourcefulness by planning and leading community service projects. Youth, ages 5-21, work together to identify local community needs and problems, to design projects to meet those needs, and to present proposals seeking funding to a grant-making board composed of youth and adult members. Caring adult volunteers support youth efforts, and local youth-serving organizations often serve as host agencies for YAR sites. For information, contact YAR staff at NCPC, or at the Indianapolis office at 317-920-2564, or visit the YAR Web site at www.yar.org.

Visit the NCPC Web Site

The National Crime Prevention Council invites you to explore its On-Line Resource Center for all kinds of useful information about crime prevention, community building, comprehensive planning, and even fun stuff for kids! www.ncpc.org.

Materials and Resources From Other Organizations

Policing a Multicultural Community, a monograph published by the **Police Executive Research Forum** as part of its Fresh Perspectives series, examines the dynamics of intergroup conflict in multicultural communities. After exploring the roots of intergroup conflict, authors Henry I. DeGeneste and John P. Sullivan assess the impact of social factors, such as migration, ethnic tension, and resource scarcity, upon community life in increasingly diverse communities. The authors combine insights gained from police practice and research to suggest practical methods for minimizing discord and building trust among the police and multicultural communities of tomorrow. With its thorough analysis of the causes and effects of cross-cultural conflict, this text complements the practical, hands-on NCPC publications on the same subject. Available from PERF Publications, PO Box 39005, Solon, OH 44139, 888-202-4563, fax: 800-669-3658.

The Refugee Service Center at the Center for Applied Linguistics (CAL) produces and distributes free and low cost refugee resource materials including an orientation handbook for refugees, fact booklets on refugee populations and cultures, and English/foreign language phrase books. CAL is an excellent resource for anyone wanting to learn about or work with refugees. For a list of CAL publications, contact La Ditthavong at CAL, 1118 22nd Street, NW, Washington, DC 20037, 202-429-9292, fax: 202-659-5641.

The National Clearinghouse for Alcohol and Drug Information provides a full on-line catalog of publications that provides information for drug and alcohol prevention, as well as referrals. 800-729-6686 or www.health.org.

The National Clearinghouse on Child Abuse and Neglect is a great source for child abuse and neglect prevention information. Its on-line catalog offers numerous publications, as well as directories that can be searched to find out about various child abuse prevention services throughout the country. The Web site also provides information about specialized services, such as statistics and child welfare. www.222.calib.com/nccanch.

Contacts

1. Individual Organizations

Resource Organizations for Service Providers

The **Corporation for National Service** encourages people to donate time to provide service to their communities. The Corporation for National Service oversees three national service initiatives, AmeriCorps, Learn and Serve, and Senior Corps.

1. AmeriCorps encourages people to become active in community service through three major programs:
   - AmeriCorps State and National Direct trains people to supply community service and enables them to train others as well.
   - AmeriCorps National Civilian Community Corps members work in teams and focus on such issues as education, public safety, and disaster relief.
   - AmeriCorps VISTA is a full-time service program in which volunteers work in nonprofit organizations and initiate service programs for the communities they serve.
2. Learn and Serve America supports teachers and adult community members and helps them involve youth in education-related community service.
3. National Senior Service Corps provides service opportunities for people over the age of 55. Some of their key programs include Foster Grandparents, Senior Companions, and Retired and Senior Volunteers.

Corporation for National Service, 1201 New York Avenue, NW, Washington, DC 20525, 202-606-5000, www.nationalservice.org.

The **Boy Scouts of America** offers a crime prevention program and a crime prevention merit badge focusing on neighborhood watch, the roles of law enforcement, and gangs. 800-323-0732.

Girl Scouts of the U.S.A. has “Girl Scouts Beyond Bars,” a program for girls to work directly with prison inmates and provide service for their families, in addition to a general violence prevention program. 800-GSU-FORU (478-3678).

The **Nonprofit Risk Management Center** helps nonprofits control risk and focus on their missions. If you have a program that provides field trips, for example, you need to protect your organization from the risk of liability in case of accidents. The Center provides technical assistance and publishes a wide range of easy-to-understand materials. Representatives of nonprofit organizations are eligible for free subscriptions to the Center's newsletter, *Community Risk Management & Insurance.* 202-785-3891, www.nonprofitrisk.org.

Public Allies offers interested young adults the opportunity to volunteer their time and efforts to provide service to needy communities. The core of the Public Allies program is the 10-month Ally Apprenticeship during which volunteers work full-time to organize community service projects. 202-822-1180.

Victim Assistance

The **National Victim Center** is dedicated to reducing the consequences of crime on victims and society by promoting victims' rights and victim assistance through training and technical assistance, a quarterly newsletter, a legislative database, toll-free information and referral, and crime victim civil litigation referral service. 2111 Wilson Boulevard, Suite 300, Arlington, VA 22201, 703-276-2880.

The **National Organization for Victim Assistance** (NOVA) works to implement services and achieve recognition of victims' rights. NOVA provides training, technical assistance, and direct service to crime victims and maintains an information clearinghouse on issues related to victimization. 1757 Park Road, NW, Washington, DC 20010, 202-232-6682.

Domestic Violence

Family Violence Prevention Fund/Health Resource Center provides information on treating and preventing family violence and referrals to local resources. In addition, the Fund developed the Health Resource Center to provide family violence information to health care providers. The Center's hotline, 1-888-Rx-ABUSE, serves to help improve the health care response to domestic violence.

The **National Domestic Violence Hotline** provides emergency services and referrals for domestic violence victims and service providers in as many as 139 languages. 800-799-SAFE.

Child Abuse

National Network of Children's Advocacy Centers provides multidisciplinary technical assistance, training, and other resources to communities for child abuse prevention. Contributing disciplines include law enforcement, medical health services, victim advocacy, and child protective services. 800-239-9950.

2. Federal Agencies

The U.S. Department of Justice

The **Office of Justice Programs** is composed of a number of bureaus, several of which offer services and programs that would be useful in developing refugee crime prevention programs. United States Department of Justice, 810 7th Street, NW, Washington, DC 20531

- The **Bureau of Justice Assistance** provides technical assistance and training to community groups and local governments to assist in reducing violent crime and substance abuse and to promote community prevention programs. 800-688-4252.
- The **Office of Juvenile Justice and Delinquency Prevention** provides resources and support to combat juvenile delinquency, especially gang violence, and initiates programs to prevent child abuse. 202-307-5911.
- The **Office for Victims of Crime** provides funding for victim services and trainings. A unique aspect of this agency is that funding comes from fines, bail forfeitures, and penalties paid by criminal offenders. 800-627-6872.
- The **Violence Against Women Grants Office** offers grant funding to organizations that assist victimized women and promotes outreach programs. 202-307-6026.
- The **Executive Office for Weed and Seed** supports the development of community-based crime prevention. Its goal is to "weed" crime and violence from communities through community oriented policing programs and to "seed" healthier communities through neighborhood rejuvenation. 202-616-1152. For a newsletter, call 202-616-1152.

Immigration and Naturalization Services administers U.S. immigration and naturalization laws. It provides assistance through community voluntary agencies' training and instruction that facilitate immigrants' compliance with legal requirements for residency and citizenship. U.S. Department of Justice, 425 I Street, NW, Washington, DC 20536, 202-616-7762.

The **Community Relations Service** provides dispute mediation to communities experiencing racial or cultural strife. It is a sponsor of the Southeast Asian POST program in California. 5550 Friendship Boulevard, Suite 330, Chevy Chase, MD 20815, 301-492-5929.

The U.S. Department of Health and Human Services

The **Office of Refugee Resettlement (ORR),** Administration for Children and Families at the United States Department of Health and

Human Services is the primary federal agency responsible for refugee assistance in the United States. It has funded demonstration and service projects to improve relationships between refugees and the law enforcement community. ORR, 370 L'Enfant Promenade, SW, 6th Floor, Washington, DC 20447 or visit the Web site www.acf.dhhs.gov/programs/orr.

The **Administration on Children, Youth, and Families (ACYF)** has a number of programs focusing on runaway and homeless youth. ACYF, 370 C Street, NW, Room 2428, Washington, DC 20201, 202-205-8102.

3. National Law Enforcement Organizations

The **Community Policing Consortium** is a partnership of five of the leading police organizations in the United States (listed below) and is administered and funded by the U.S. Department of Justice, Office of Community Oriented Policing Services (COPS). Its mission is to deliver training to COPS grantees and disseminate innovative publications focusing on the latest developments in community policing. The Consortium can be reached at 1726 M Street, NW, Suite 801, Washington, DC 20036, 800-833-3085 or www.communitypolicing.org.

- The **International Association of Chiefs of Police (IACP)** is an international membership organization of law enforcement executives that develops policy, offers advocacy and training, and publishes information on the full range of policing issues. 515 North Washington Street, Alexandria, VA 22314-2357, 800-843-4227.
- The **Police Executive Research Forum** is a national membership organization dedicated to improving policing and advancing professionalism through research and involvement in public policy debate. It provides an extensive number of publications on a wide range of law enforcement topics, such as community policing. 1120 Connecticut Avenue, NW, Suite 930, Washington, DC 20036, 202-466-7820 or 888-202-4563.
- The **National Sheriffs' Association** provides training, research, technical assistance, and publications and sponsors a number of programs, including Neighborhood Watch and the National Sheriffs' Institute. 1450 Duke Street, Alexandria, VA 22201, 703-836-7827.
- The **National Organization of Black Law Enforcement Executives** (NOBLE) focuses on improving law enforcement administration and implementing programs to prevent crime and violence, as well as offering trainings, employment services, research, and publications. 4609 Pinecrest Office Park Drive, Suite F, Alexandria, VA 22312, 703-658-1529.

- The **Police Foundation** is dedicated to supporting innovation and improvement in policing through its research, technical assistance, and communications programs. The Foundation conducts seminal research in police behavior, policy, and procedure and works to transfer to local agencies the best new information about practices for dealing effectively with a range of important police operational and administrative concerns. 1001 22nd Street, NW, Suite 200, Washington, DC 20037, 202-833-1460.

4. National Refugee Organizations

National Refugee Networks

The national refugee networks are service organizations initiated and run by refugees. Each national organization has local affiliates known as Mutual Assistance Associations (MAAs) located in many communities around the United States. These MAAs are staffed by refugees of a specific ethnicity and can be key community partners. Get in touch with these agencies to find out if there are ethnic community-based organizations in your locality.

Cambodian Network Council
713 D Street, SE
Washington, DC 20003
(phone) 202-546-9144
(fax) 202-546-9147

Cuban Exodus Relief Fund
7300 NW 35th Terrace
Miami, FL 33122
(phone) 305-592-7768
(fax) 305-592-7889

Haitian Centers Council, Inc.
50 Court Street, #1010
Brooklyn, NY 11201
(phone) 718-855-7275
(fax) 718-852-5377

Kurdish Human Rights Watch
10560 Main Street, Suite 205
Fairfax, VA 22030
(phone) 703-385-3806
(fax) 703-385-3643

Cuban American National Foundation
1000 Thomas Jefferson Street, NW
Washington, DC 20007
(phone) 202-265-2822
(fax) 202-338-0308

Ethiopian Community Development Council
1036 South Highland Street
Arlington, VA 22204
(phone) 703-685-0510
(fax) 703-685-0529

Hmong National Development, Inc.
1326 18th Street, NW, Suite 200-A
Washington, DC 20036
(phone) 202-463-2118
(fax) 202-463-2119

Laotian Humanitarian Foundation
PO Box 237
Long Beach, CA 90801
(phone) 714-824-4549
(fax) 310-804-3900

Montagard/Dega Association International
3100-I Summit Avenue
Greensboro, NC 27405
(phone) 910-375-4223 or 8190
(fax) 910-375-5614

Somali Benadir Community
c/o Virginia Council of Churches
1214 West Graham Road, Suite 3
Richmond, VA 23220
(phone) 804-321-3305
(fax) 804-329-5066

National Association of Vietnamese American Services Agencies
1628 16th Street, NW, 3rd Floor
Washington, DC 20009
(phone) 202-667-4690
(fax) 202-667-6449

Southeast Asia Resource Action Center
1628 16th Street, NW, 3rd Floor
Washington, DC 20009
(phone) 202-667-4690
(fax) 202-667-6449

Voluntary Agencies (VOLAGs)

The national VOLAGs take responsibility for assisting new refugees in settling into their new communities successfully. Each national organization has affiliates located in many communities around the United States. The affiliates can also serve as excellent community partners. Get in touch with these agencies to find the affiliates in your community, or look them up in the telephone directory.

Church World Service Immigration and Refugee Program
475 Riverside Drive, Room 666
New York, NY 10115-0050
(phone) 212-870-3300
(fax) 212-870-2055

Immigration and Refugee Services of America (IRSA)
U.S. Community for Refugees
1717 Massachusetts Avenue, NW, Suite 701
Washington, DC 20036
(phone) 202-347-3507
(fax) 202-347-3418

Lutheran Immigration and Refugee Services
390 Park Avenue South
New York, NY 10016-8803
(phone) 212-532-6350
(fax) 212-683-1329

World Relief Refugee Services
201 Route 9 W North
Congers, NY 10920
(phone) 914-268-4135, ext. 18
(fax) 914-268-2271

Episcopal Migration Ministries The Episcopal Church Center
815 Second Avenue, 5th Floor
New York, NY 10017
(phone) 212-867-8400
(fax) 212-490-6684

International Rescue Committee
122 East 42nd Street, 12th Floor
New York, NY 10168-1289
(phone) 212-551-3000
(fax) 212-551-3180

United States Catholic Conference Migration and Refugee Service
3211 Fourth Street, NE
Washington, DC 20017-1194
(phone) 202-541-3220
(fax) 202-541-3399

State Refugee Coordinators

Within each state government there is an office responsible for helping refugees and all New Americans. The head of this office, the state refugee coordinator, is familiar with the demographics and needs of the refugees throughout the state and can help you identify community leaders and service providers in any given community. Here is contact information for each of these offices.

ALABAMA
Department of Human Resources
South Gordon Persons Building
50 Ripley Street
Montgomery, AL 36130
(phone) 334-242-1773
(fax) 334-242-0513

ALASKA
St. Mary's Church
2222 East Tudor Road
Anchorage, AK 99507
(phone) 907-563-3341
(fax) 907-562-2202

ARKANSAS
Division of Human Services
Slot # 1224
PO Box 1437
Little Rock, AR 72203-1437
(phone) 501-682-8263
(fax) 501-682-1597

ARIZONA
Department of Economic Security
Community Services Administration
PO Box 6123 - Site Code 086Z
Phoenix, AZ 85005
(phone) 602-542-6600
(fax) 602-542-6400

CALIFORNIA
Refugee Program Bureau
744 P Street, MS 6-646
Sacramento, CA 95814
(phone) 916-654-6379
(fax) 916-654-7187

CALIFORNIA
Department of Social Services
744 P Street, MS 17 - 11
Sacramento, CA 95814
(phone) 916-657-2598
(fax) 916-654-6012

COLORADO
Department of Social Services
Colorado Refugee Services Program
789 Sherman, Suite 250
Denver, CO 80203
(phone) 303-863-8216, ext. 308
(fax) 303-863-0838

CONNECTICUT
Department of Social Services
Special Programs Division
25 Sigourney Street
Hartford, CT 06106
(phone) 860-424-5381
(fax) 860-424-4957

DELAWARE
Division of Social Services
Herman M. Holloway Sr. Campus
1901 North Dupont Highway
PO Box 906, Lewis Building
New Castle, DE 19720
(phone) 302-577-4453
(fax) 302-577-4405

DISTRICT OF COLUMBIA
Office of Refugee Resettlement
Department of Human Services
65 I Street, SW, Room 217
Washington, DC 20024
(phone) 202-724-4820

FLORIDA
Department of Children and Rehabilitative Services
Building 2, Room 202
1317 Winewood Boulevard
Tallahassee, FL 32399-0700
(phone) 904-488-3791
(fax) 904-487-4272

GEORGIA
Department of Human Resources
DFC/DFCS - Community Programs
2 Peachtree Street, 12th Floor, Suite 404
Atlanta, GA 30303-3180
(phone) 404-657-3428
(fax) 404-657-3489

HAWAII
Office of Community Services
830 Punchebowl Street, Room 420
Honolulu, HI 96813
(phone) 808-586-8675
(fax) 808-586-8685

IDAHO
Bureau of Family Self Support
450 West State Street, 6th Floor
PO Box 83720, Towers Building
Boise, ID 83720
(phone) 208-336-5533, ext. 262
(fax) 208-336-0880

ILLINOIS
Refugee Resettlement Program
Illinois Department of Public Aid
527 South Wells, Suite 500
Chicago, IL 60607
(phone) 312-793-7120
(fax) 312-793-2281

INDIANA
FSSA, Family and Children's Division
402 West Washington Street
Room W-363
Indianapolis, IN 46204
(phone) 765-282-4919
(fax) 765-232-4615

KANSAS
Department of Social and Rehabilitation Services
Smith-Wilson Building
300 SW Oakley
Topeka, KS 66606
(phone) 785-368-8115
(fax) 785-296-6960

KENTUCKY
Catholic Charities of Louisville
2911 South Fourth Street
Louisville, KY 40208
(phone) 502-637-9786
(fax) 502-637-9780

LOUISIANA
Contracts Management and Evaluation
Department of Social Services
1001 Howard Avenue, Suite 1735
New Orleans, LA 70113
(phone) 504-568-8958
(fax)504-599-0931

MAINE
Bureau of Social Services, Dept of Human Services
State House Station 11
221 State Street
Augusta, ME 04333
(phone) 207-287-5060
(fax) 207-287-5031

MARYLAND
Maryland Office of New Americans
Department Of Human Resources
Saratoga State Center
311 West Saratoga Street, Room 222
Baltimore, MD 21201
(phone) 410-767-7021
(fax) 410-333-0079

MASSACHUSETTS
Office for Refugee and Immigrants
18 Tremont Street, Suite 600
Boston, MA 02108
(phone) 617-727-8190
(fax) 617-727-1822

MICHIGAN
Refugee Assistance Division
Department of Social Services
235 South Grand Avenue, Suite 1013
Lansing, MI 48909
(phone) 517-335-6358
(fax) 517-241-7943

MINNESOTA
Refugee and Immigration Assistance Division
Human Services Building, 3rd Floor
444 Lafayette Road
St. Paul, MN 55155
(phone) 612-296-1383
(fax) 612-297-5840

MISSISSIPPI
Division of Family and Children's Services
PO Box 352
750 North State Street
Jackson, MS 39202
(phone) 601-359-4982
(fax) 601-359-4978

MISSOURI
Division of Family Services
Refugee Resettlement Program
2705 West Main
PO Box 88
Jefferson City, MO 65103
(phone) 573-526-5605
(fax) 573-526-5592

MONTANA
Department of Social Work
University of Montana
Missoula, MT 59812
(phone) 406-243-2336
(fax) 406-243-4076

NEBRASKA
Department of Health and Human Services
PO Box 95044
Lincoln, NE 68504
(phone) 402-471-9200
(fax) 402-471-9455
(E-mail) MDIAZ@hhs.state.ne.us

NEVADA
Catholic Community Services of Nevada
1501 Las Vegas Boulevard North
Las Vegas, NV 89101
(phone) 702-383-8387
(fax) 702-385-7748

NEW HAMPSHIRE
Governor's Office of Energy and Community Services
57 Regional Drive
Concord, NH 03301
(phone) 603-271-2611
(fax) 603-271-2615

NEW JERSEY
Department of Human Services
Division of Youth and Family Services
50 East State Street - CN 717
Trenton, NJ 08625
(phone) 609-984-3154
(fax) 609-292-8224

NEW JERSEY
Department of Human Services
Division of Youth and Family
50 East State Street - CN 717
Trenton, NJ 08625
(phone) 609-292-8395
(fax) 609-292-8224

NEW YORK
Office of Refugee Immigration and Special Services
40 North Pearl Street
10th Street, Section B
Albany, NY 12243
(phone) 518-402-3096
(fax) 518-402-3029

NORTH CAROLINA
Family Services Section
Department of Human Resources
325 North Salisbury Street
Ralcigh, NC 27603
(phone) 919-733-3677
(fax) 919-715-0023

NORTH DAKOTA
Department of Human Services,
Children and Family Division
600 East Boulevard Avenue, Judicial Wing
State Capitol, 3rd Floor
Bismarck, ND 58505
(phone) 701-328-4934
(fax) 701-328-2359

OHIO
Department of Human Services
65 East State Street, 5th Floor
Columbus, OH 43215
(phone) 614-466-0995
(fax) 614-466-0164

OKLAHOMA
Family Support Service Division
PO Box 25352
Oklahoma City, OK 73125
(phone) 405-521-4091
(fax) 405-521-4158

OREGON
Department of Human Resources
100 Public Service Building
500 Summer Street NE
2nd Floor North
Salem, OR 97310
(phone) 503-645-6093
(fax) 503-378-3782

PENNSYLVANIA
Department of Public Welfare
Office of Social Programs
1401 North 7th Street, 2nd Floor
Bertolini Building
Harrisburg, PA 17105
(phone) 717-783-2093
(fax) 717-772-1529

RHODE ISLAND
Department of Human Services
275 Westminster Mall, 4th Floor
Providence, RI 02903
(phone) 401-222-2551
(fax) 401-222-2595

SOUTH CAROLINA
Department of Social Services
PO Box 1520
Columbia, SC 29202
(phone) 803-734-5916
(fax) 803-734-6093

SOUTH DAKOTA
Department of Social Services
Kniep Building
700 Governor's Drive
Pierre, SD 57501
(phone) 605-773-4678
(fax)605-773-6834

TENNESSEE
Department of Human Services
Community Assistance Services
400 Deaderick Street, 14th Floor
Nashville, TN 37209
(phone) 615-313-4761
(fax) 615-532-9956

TEXAS
Texas Department of Human Services
701 West 51st Street, Mail Code W-619
Austin, TX 78714-9030
(phone) 512-438-5545
(fax) 512-438-3884

UTAH
Department of Workforce Services
1385 South State Street
Salt Lake City, UT 84115
(phone) 801-468-0089
(fax) 801-468-0160

VERMONT
Agency of Human Services
108 Cherry Street
PO Box 70
Burlington, VT 05402
(phone) 802-651-1874
(fax) 802-865-7754

VIRGINIA
Department of Social Services
Office of Newcomer Services
730 East Broad Street
Richmond, VA 23219-1849
(phone) 804-692-1206
(fax) 804-692-2215

WASHINGTON
Department of Social and Health Services
Office of Immigrant and Refugee Assistance
1009 College Street
PO Box 45420
Olympia, WA 95804
(phone) 360-413-3213
(fax) 360-413-3494

WEST VIRGINIA
Office of Family Support
DHHR, Capitol Complex
Building 6, Room 749
Charleston, WV 25305
(phone) 304-558-8290
(fax) 304-558-2059

WISCONSIN
Department of Workforce Development
131 West Wilson Street, Room 802
Madison, WI 53703
(phone) 608-266-0578
(fax) 608-267-4897

WYOMING
Administrative Services Division
Department of Family Services
Hathaway Building, Room 352
Cheyenne, WY 82002
(phone) 307-777-6081
(fax) 307-777-7747

Internet Resources

Communities Against Violence Network (Cavnet) is a virtual library of information about domestic violence. It provides names of organizations, journals, articles and links to many important violence prevention resources. Cavnet also allows you to submit information in order to get your organization's message about domestic violence out to the public. **www.asksam.com/cavnet/**

The **Community Policing Consortium** Web page provides information about training sessions and training curriculum on community policing initiatives, as well as model programs like the ones in this book and general information and materials useful for community policing programs. It also provides links to other related Web sites. **www.communitypolicing.com**

DiversityRX is a great resource for anyone doing work with refugees and diversity. Diversity RX promotes language and cultural competence to improve the quality of health care provided to ethnically diverse communities. This Web site also provides several links to other cross-cultural and diversity resources on the Web. **www.DiversityRX.org**

The **Family Violence Prevention Fund** Web site provides facts and prevention solutions for combating domestic violence, health care responses to domestic violence, and personal stories of domestic violence survivors. The Web site even has a quiz you can take to test your knowledge of domestic violence. **www.fvpf.org/fund/index.html**

The **National Center For Community Policing** provides training and technical assistance for community policing programs, as well as publications and articles concerning successful community policing programs. **www.ssc.msu.edu/~cj/cp/cptoc.html**

The **National Crime Prevention Council** Web site details the organization and provides useful crime prevention information for law enforcement officials, service providers, and government officials. The NCPC Web site also provides information about conferences and trainings offered throughout the United States. **www.ncpc.org**

The **National Criminal Justice Reference Service** provides information about crime and drug prevention, law enforcement research, and victim evaluations. **www.ncjrs.org**

Look for information about **ORR** and its programs and services on its Web site. **www.acf.dhhs.gov/programs/orr**

Partnerships Against Violence Network (Pavnet) is a "one-stop" searchable resource of information about violence prevention. Partnered with the U.S. Department of Education, Agriculture, Labor, Justice, Defense, HHS, and HUD, Pavnet offers a unique compilation of violence prevention information. **www.pavnet.org/**

Streetbeat has valuable information about community policing on this informative and interactive Web site. The Web page also provides many links that will be beneficial to law enforcement officers. **www.nlectc.org**

The Washington State Institute for Community Oriented Policing (WSICOP) provides information about community policing and training and also has links to police departments with Web pages, as well as several police related sites. **www.idi.wsu.edu/wsicop/**

The **U.S. Committee for Refugees** provides statistics and information about refugees and their situations around the world on its Web site. **www.refugees.org**

Glossary of Terms and Abbreviations

Terms

Asylee

Aslyees get to the United States first, then ask for "refuge." Refugees just cross the border out of their country and usually try to get to United Nations High Commissioner for Refugees for status determination.

The main difference between a refugee and an asylum seeker is where they are when they apply for refuge.

Amerasian

Amerasian in common usage refers to a person who has one parent (usually the mother) who is (Southeast) Asian, often Vietnamese, and one parent who is "American."

Entrant

Cubans and Haitians are generally not granted either of the above technical statuses but given the legal term Cuban Haitian "Entrant."

Immigrant

A person living permanently in a country of which his or her family is not native. Refugees, asylees, entrants, and Amerasians are special categories of immigrants.

Law enforcement officer

Includes sworn law enforcement staff, such as police, sheriff's department officers, community relations officers; crime prevention officers; police detectives and criminal investigators; and non-sworn staff working for a law enforcement agency in a police-like capacity, such as community liaisons, community policing assistants, community service officers, and public affairs assistants; prosecutors, district attorneys, and other legal staff; judges and other court personnel; and corrections, parole, and probation officers.

Refugee

A person seeking refuge who has left or escaped from his or her own country because of a fear of persecution because of race, religion, nationality, membership in a particular social group, or political opinion.

Refugees are considered for resettlement from outside of the country they wish to enter. When a person has entered a country and they seek to stay for their safety, we call them "asylum seekers" or asylees.

The Weed and Seed initiative is one of the longest-running community-based programs of the Office of Justice Programs, U.S. Department of Justice. The Weed and Seed strategy consists of four elements:

1. Coordinated law enforcement to "weed" crime, drug, and gang activity;
2. Community oriented policing to serve as a bridge between the "weeding" (law enforcement) and "seeding" efforts (crime prevention and neighborhood restoration);
3. Prevention, intervention, and treatment to increase the availability and coordination of human services—such as drug and crime prevention programs, educational opportunities, drug treatment, family services, and recreational activities for youth; and
4. Neighborhood restoration to revitalize distressed neighborhoods and improve the quality of life for Weed and Seed residents through economic development, job opportunities, improved housing conditions, and increased access to affordable housing.

For further information, contact the Executive Office of Weed and Seed at 202-616-1152.

Abbreviations

ESL—English as a Second Language

MAA—Mutual Assistance Association, a community-based organization initiated and administered by refugees to provide services for refugees.

P.O.S.T.—Peace Officer Standards and Training Council

VOLAG—Voluntary Agency, also known as private voluntary organization (PVO), is a national organization with the mission of assisting refugee reception and placement in the United States and coordinating service provision to refugees on the local level once they have arrived in communities in the United States.

Successful Strategy

Do you have a successful refugee crime prevention strategy that others should know about?

If you do, the National Crime Prevention Council wants to hear about it. Just complete and fax this page to (202) 785-0698 attn Outreach to New Americans staff. Outreach to New Americans staff will get in touch with you to explain the submission process.

Selected strategies will be showcased on our Web site so that as many individuals and organizations as possible will be able to take advantage of the best ideas available.

NAME

PROJECT NAME

ORGANIZATION

ADDRESS

( ) ( )

PHONE FAX

E-MAIL

TAKE A BITE OUT OF

CRIME®